Leaders of the Digital Age

Arzu Uğurlu Kara / Murat Sağbaş (eds.)

Leaders of the Digital Age

Strategies for Managing the Future

PETER LANG

Berlin · Bruxelles · Chennai · Lausanne · Oxford · New York

Bibliographic Information published by the Deutsche Nationalbibliothek
The Deutsche Nationalbibliothek lists this publication in the Deutsche Nationalbibliografie; detailed bibliographic data is available in the internet at http://dnb.d-nb.de.

Library of Congress Cataloging-in-Publication Data

Names: Uğurlu Kara, Arzu, author. | Sağbaş, Murat, author.
Title: Leader of the digital age : strategies for managing the future / edited by Arzu Uğurlu Kara and Murat Sağbaş.
Description: New York : Peter Lang, [2025] | Includes bibliographical references.
Identifiers: LCCN 2025004132 (print) | LCCN 2025004133 (ebook) | ISBN 9783631931325 (paperback) | ISBN 9783631936429 (ebook) | ISBN 9783631936436 (epub)
Subjects: LCSH: Leadership—Technological innovations. | Industrial management.
Classification: LCC HD57.7 .U37 2025 (print) | LCC HD57.7 (ebook) | DDC 658.4/092—dc23/eng/20250331
LC record available at https://lccn.loc.gov/2025004132
LC ebook record available at https://lccn.loc.gov/2025004133

ISBN 978-3-631-93132-5 (Print)
ISBN 978-3-631-93642-9 (E-PDF)
ISBN 978-3-631-93643-6 (E-PUB)
DOI 10.3726/10.3726/b22819

Published by Peter Lang GmbH, Berlin (Germany)

info@peterlang.com

This publication has been peer reviewed.

www.peterlang.com

Foreword

The digital age marks a period of profound transformation for organizations and leadership paradigms, one that is defined by rapidly changing dynamics. In a world where technology is increasingly integrated into business practices, traditional leadership models often fall short. This book aims to explore the impact of digital leadership on organizations and highlight how this transformation is reshaping leadership, culture, strategy, and key business functions.

"Leaders of the Digital Age: Strategies for Managing the Future" delves deeply into the various aspects of digital leadership, examining its profound influence on organizational structures and business processes. Each chapter offers a comprehensive analysis of how digital leadership impacts organizational strategies, human resource management, innovation, and crisis management. The book particularly addresses the competencies required for leaders to adapt to the fast-paced and complex environment of the digital age.

This book underscores that digital leadership is not only about technology and tools but also entails a human-centered approach. It emphasizes that digital leaders must possess critical skills to manage organizational culture, drive sustainable change, enhance employee performance, and make quick, effective decisions during times of crisis. Additionally, the role of digital leadership in fostering organizational innovation, strategic communication, and digital learning environments is explored in depth.

Far beyond being an academic text, this book seeks to serve as a practical guide for leaders, managers, and professionals who are undergoing organizational transformation. It explores the essential strategic management skills required to thrive in the digital age and addresses the ethical and societal responsibilities that digital leaders must navigate. The challenges faced by digital leaders in the transformation process, along with strategies for overcoming them, are laid out to provide readers with a clear roadmap.

There is no doubt that mastering digital leadership is essential for success in today's dynamic and VUCA (Volatility, Uncertainty, Complexity, Ambiguity) world. In this context, digital leadership goes beyond merely utilizing technology; it involves making decisions that propel organizations forward and ensuring their success in the future. This book comprehensively examines how leaders can be effective in the digital world, and how they can foster organizational success and sustainable change.

This work aims to be not only an academic resource but also a valuable guide for anyone navigating the complexities of digital leadership. By exploring the various dimensions of digital leadership in depth, it aspires to be an essential reference for both the academic and practical realms. It will serve as a key resource for every leader seeking to harness the power of digital transformation and move confidently into the future.

Editors

Contents

1

Digital Leadership and Its Integration into Organizational Culture

Leading Sustainable Change, Competences, and Culture

Sebahattin Kılınç[1] *& Murat Sağbaş*[2]

1. Introduction

Digital leadership empowers subordinates' digital capabilities and promotes the use of digital environments and technologies in line with a specific digital strategy to complete or advance a business's digital transformation. Developing a digital strategy necessitates digital competencies, literacy, and an understanding of barriers and opportunities in digitalizing business models. Organizational culture reflects unwritten behavioral patterns and is influenced by factors such as geography, leadership style, organizational history, external environment, and employee values. A pro-technology stance is one such factor, indicating an open and transparent organizational culture. Digital leadership involves guiding and motivating subordinates within digital environments to achieve digital transformation. This process requires continuity and sustainability, necessitating that organization members possess digital skills and understand the purposes of digital technologies. Digital leaders foster a participative and democratic atmosphere, encouraging open expression of opinions. They prioritize digital education and continuously organize training programs to enhance their employees' skills.

2. Key Dimensions of Digital Leadership

Digital leadership extends beyond technological expertise to include the ability to guide and inspire through digital transformation. This leadership

1 Assoc. Prof., National Defense University, <kujase69@gmail.com>.
2 Assoc. Prof. National Defense University, <muratsagbass@gmail.com>

type is closely tied to organizational structure, influencing and being influenced by frameworks, hierarchies, and cultural norms. Effective digital leaders bridge the gap between traditional practices and the digital world's demands, aiding organizations in adapting to technological changes while preserving core values (Johari & Hendra, 2023). Key dimensions include competency, organizational strategy, and the integration of transformational and distributed leadership principles (Ming & Mansor, 2024). Digital leadership also involves creating a vision that integrates technology into business strategy, fostering an innovative culture, developing employee skills, focusing on customers, and ensuring organizational flexibility (Kawiana, 2023). It is grounded in digital insights, decision-making, implementation, and guidance, with digital thinking as the foundation (Peng, 2021). Khurniawan et al. (2024) highlight competencies like digital literacy, vision, advocacy, presence, communication, adaptability, self-awareness, and cultural awareness as essential in addressing digital transformation challenges. These competencies enable leaders to effectively guide teams, foster innovation, and align digital strategies with business objectives. Henderikx and Stoffers (2022) emphasize the importance of subcentric leadership, which supports intergenerational and cross-cultural teamwork by fostering commitment and loyalty among diverse individuals. Historically, leadership was seen as a heroic model with proactive leaders shaping the future through top-down directives (Fletcher, 2004). However, a shift to shared responsibility and distributed leadership enhances organizational agility, fosters innovation, and enables adaptation to dynamic environments. In digital contexts, leaders must create environments that encourage experimentation and co-creation, leveraging collective intelligence to boost creativity and cultivate continuous learning, essential for navigating digital transformation complexities (Solheim & Skjølsvik, 2022).

3. Digital Competences

Digital transformation has reshaped the workplace and redefined the essential skills and competencies for success. Literature on digital leadership suggests that digital leaders must have networking intelligence, enabling them to build networks both technically and organizationally, and develop new business models for the digital era (Musaigwa & Kalitanyi, 2023). These changes present significant challenges for individuals and organizations. Barling et al. (2008) highlight two themes linked to digital competence: individual behaviors in organizations are influenced by biological, social, and organizational factors, and the gap between theory and practice is closing due to digital tools. Digital competence allows individuals to utilize these tools for problem-solving and innovation, serving as a bridge between technology and practical application in various contexts. Digital competence includes skills beyond mere technological proficiency, such as critical thinking, problem-solving, and effectively navigating digital information. As digital technologies evolve, the importance of digital competence in education, workforce development, and civic participation will likely increase. The DigComp Framework (2022) provides a structured approach to digital competence, covering five areas: information and data literacy, communication and collaboration, digital content creation, safety, and problem-solving. Each area includes specific competencies with proficiency levels from foundational to specialized, outlining the knowledge, skills, and attitudes necessary for digital competence. This framework aids in promoting lifelong learning and active societal engagement. Technology leadership must not only facilitate communication but also drive innovation and competitive advantage through a visionary and strategic approach (Dey, 2022). Aligning technology initiatives with business goals through open communication and collaboration is crucial for organizational innovation and competitiveness. Effective leaders must consider ethical aspects of digital communication, ensuring inclusivity and accessibility. Adapting communication styles to diverse audiences and platforms, along with facilitating knowledge sharing and problem-solving in virtual environments, are key components of digital leadership. Leaders must understand the capabilities and limitations of various technologies while aligning digital initiatives with broader strategic objectives.

4. Digital Leadership Strategies

Effective digital leadership requires both technical skills and the ability to adapt to evolving demands while guiding teams empathetically and transparently through complex changes. Critical problem-solving and decision-making skills are essential for overcoming challenges and driving strategic initiatives. Key strategies include clear communication for organizational alignment, empathy to understand team needs, and effective delegation to enhance productivity and accountability (Sheninger, 2019). Honesty, consistency, and integrity are crucial for building trust and respect, while inspiring and motivating teams are vital for high performance and engagement. A strategic vision is a guiding principle for digital transformation, ensuring alignment with long-term goals (Pieretto & Hinterhuber, 2021). Developing this vision involves assessing digital maturity and identifying areas for impactful transformation by analyzing existing processes to pinpoint where digital solutions add the most value. However, a robust digital vision also requires leveraging technologies in a competitive context. Strategies for IT integration into marketing and operations are crucial for enhancing communication, optimizing strategies, and driving innovation. A comprehensive digital strategy across all business areas is key to sustainable competitive advantage by recognizing and addressing the challenges and opportunities of digitalization (Becker & Schmid, 2020). Prioritizing the development of specific digital capabilities is essential, as organizations cannot invest in all areas simultaneously (Salamzadeh, 2024). Maturity models provide a framework to measure digital capabilities across technology, processes, and human resources (Duncan et al., 2022). Additionally, fostering a collaborative environment where cross-functional teams share knowledge and best practices is vital for developing digital capabilities (Brunner et al., 2023). Training programs, including workshops, online courses, mentoring, and hands-on training tailored to employee needs, are part of the upskilling and reskilling process. In developing countries, integrating technology into HR practices can improve organizational performance and employee well-being (Alhmoud & AlKasasbeh, 2024). However, relying solely on technology without considering the human aspect risks creating a disconnect. The digital divide and resistance to change can exacerbate inequalities and hinder technology adoption (Springs, 2024). Initial disruptions caused by AI in healthcare suggest that technological leadership alone may not mitigate effects on productivity, indicating the need for a balanced approach that considers human factors (Alenezi et al., 2024). Implementing user-centered design in HR (Maulana Prawiro & Rosi Subhiyakto, 2024) and aligning HR technology with organizational strategies highlight the importance of balanced leadership.

5. Organizational Culture and Change

Organizational culture generally involves an organization's values as reflected in its norms, artifacts, and behaviors (Homburg & Pflesser, 2000). It can be visualized as an iceberg, with visible aspects like behaviors and language, and a larger, hidden component of attitudes and perceptions influencing performance. The challenge in defining organizational culture arises from not distinguishing its levels, as Schein (1992) notes. Schein sees organizational culture as rooted in fundamental assumptions developed over time through external adaptation and internal integration challenges. These assumptions, validated through effective group actions, form the organization's identity. Ogbonna (1992) further identifies the core components of organizational culture, describing it as "the integration of the individual into a community and the intertwining of collective programming that distinguishes the individual's mind," emphasizing shared values, norms, beliefs, and customs within a group. From a psychodynamic perspective, organizational culture is often viewed as a tool for enhancing quality and productivity. However, Schein argues that culture reflects deeply ingrained beliefs and assumptions that are not easily manipulated by management. He suggests culture evolves organically from shared experiences and collective learning. The introduction of information technologies often necessitates a cultural shift toward adaptability and a growth mindset, with leaders fostering supportive environments (Bozkus, 2024). Leaders can shape the desired culture through modeling, socializing, teaching, and responding to member behavior.

6. Sustainable Digital Change

Sustainability in the context of digital transformation addresses the continuity and resilience of digital change in organizations. Digital sustainability entails that modifications to systems, processes, and leadership strategies are consistently maintained, adapted, and evolved over time to meet the changing needs of the organization and the digital environment. In this context, sustainable change refers to the process by which an organization continuously adapts and renews itself for long-term success and growth. Sustainable change increases adaptability, while organizational adaptability contributes to the successful implementation of change initiatives. Leadership strategies play a crucial role in promoting resilience and sustainability as they influence organizations' commitment to sustainable practices (Alibašić, 2018). This leadership-driven approach to sustainability creates an environment where adaptability becomes a core organizational competency, enabling firms to respond proactively to external pressures and changes. Effective knowledge management practices significantly increase the sustainability of technology-driven enterprises, particularly in emerging markets. For instance, cloud computing and other sustainable IT infrastructures optimize the utilization of energy and computing resources, reducing both energy consumption and operational costs (Evans et al., 2017). Sustainable change and risk management exhibit a symbiotic relationship. Sustainable risk management (SRM) practices constitute an essential framework for leadership and compliance, in conjunction with a robust risk culture, appropriate risk management tools, and effective business continuity planning (Aziz & Manab, 2019). Recognizing sustainability as a corporate issue requires a focus on the core values and employee behaviors that constitute the corporate culture (Olafsen et al., 2020). When organizations commit to sustainable practices, they inherently foster a culture that values flexibility and adaptability, which are crucial for long-term survival and economic sustainability. This cultural shift not only enhances employee engagement but also cultivates a collective commitment to sustainability initiatives. Leaders who embrace sustainability values can inspire employees to adopt similar attitudes, thereby reinforcing a culture of sustainability throughout the organization.

7. Conclusion

Digital transformation of organizations is a complex and multifaceted process that necessitates a comprehensive approach to leadership, culture, and sustainability. As organizations encounter increasing pressure to adapt to new technologies and changing market demands, leaders must cultivate a culture that embraces flexibility, innovation, and continuous learning. Digital leadership plays a crucial role in this transformation by aligning technological advancements with organizational objectives, enhancing digital literacy, and fostering a collaborative environment where employees feel empowered to contribute to digital initiatives. Leaders are instrumental in shaping this cultural transformation, fostering an environment that supports innovation, adaptability, and continuous learning. In this context, the sustainability and success of digital transformation depend on the complex relationship between the effectiveness of leadership and the compatibility of organizational culture. Digital leaders must possess not only the technical acumen to implement new technologies but also the emotional intelligence and strategic vision to guide their organizations through the cultural shifts that these technologies necessitate. This comprehensive approach will ensure that digital transformation is sustainable and aligned with the organization's long-term objectives. As demonstrated throughout this study, digital leadership extends beyond the technical management of digital tools and involves shaping an organizational culture that is receptive to experimentation, continuous learning, and distributed leadership. These elements are essential for organizations to maintain competitiveness, particularly as industries face rapid technological disruption.

References

Alenezi, A., Ibrahim, I. A., Alshammari, M. H., & Liu, X. (2024). Optimizing Nursing Productivity: Exploring the Role of Artificial Intelligence, Technology Integration, Competencies, and Leadership. Journal of Nursing Management, 2024(1). DOI:10.1155/2024/8371068

Alhmoud, B., & Al_Kasasbeh, O. (2024). Integrating Technological Innovations and Human Resource Practices for Enhancing Organizational Performance and Employee Well-being in Developing Countries. *ORGANIZE: Journal of Economics, Management and Finance*, *3*(2), 101–113. DOI:10.58355/organize.v3i2.82

Alibašić, H. (2018). Leadership strategies for embedding sustainability and resilience in organizations with an emphasis on sustainable energy. Creighton Journal of Interdisciplinary Leadership, 4(1), 17. DOI:10.17062/cjil.v4i1.63

Aziz, N. A. A., & Manab, N. A. (2019). *Meeting the Stakeholder Needs and Sustaining Business Through Sustainability Risk Management Practices: A Case Study of Malaysian Environmentally Sensitive Companies* (pp. 195–208). Springer Singapore. DOI:10.1007/978-981-13-7158-5_12

Barling, J., Clegg, S. R., & Cooper, C. L. (Eds.). (2008). The SAGE Handbook of Organizational Behavior: Volume Two: Macro Approaches (Vol. 2). Sage.

Becker, W. and Schmid, O. (2020). The right digital strategy for your business: an empirical analysis of the design and implementation of digital strategies in smes and lses. Bur–Business Research, 13(3), 985–1005. DOI:10.1007/s40685-020-00124-y

Bozkus, K. (2024). *Organizational Culture Change and Technology: Navigating the Digital Transformation*. IntechOpen. DOI:10.5772/intechopen.112903

Brunner, T., Schuster, T., & Lehmann, C. (2023). Leadership's long arm: the positive influence of digital leadership on managing technology-driven change over a strengthened service innovation capacity. Frontiers in Psychology, 14. DOI:10.3389/fpsyg.2023.988808

Dey, A. (2022). Technology Leadership: Catalyst for Organizational Success. *Journal of Economics & Management Research*, 1–3. DOI:10.47363/jesmr/2022(3)222

DigComp. (2022) Publications Office of the European Union, DigComp 2.2: The Digital Competence Framework for Citizens–With new examples of knowledge, skills and attitudes. *The European Digital Competence Framework*, <https://publications.jrc.ec.europa.eu/repository/handle/JRC128415>

Duncan, R., Eden, R., Woods, L., Wong, I., & Sullivan, C. (2022). Synthesizing dimensions of digital maturity in hospitals: systematic review. Journal of Medical Internet Research, 24(3), e32994. DOI:10.2196/32994

Evans, S., Vladimirova, D., Holgado, M., Van Fossen, K., Yang, M., Silva, E. A., & Barlow, C. Y. (2017). Business model innovation for sustainability: Towards a unified perspective for creation of sustainable business models. Business strategy and the environment, 26(5), 597–608.

Fletcher, J. K. (2004). The paradox of post heroic leadership: An essay on gender, power, and transformational change. The Leadership Quarterly, 15(5), 647–661.

Henderikx, M., & Stoffers, J. (2022). An exploratory literature study into digital transformation and leadership: Toward future-proof middle managers. Sustainability, 14(2), 687.

Homburg, C., & Pflesser, C. (2000). A multiple-layer model of market-oriented organizational culture: Measurement issues and performance outcomes. Journal of Marketing Research, 37(4), 449–462.

Johari, S., & Hendra, S. (2023). An Overview of Digital Leadership Dimensions in Construction Industry. International Journal of Business and Technology Management, 5(2), 49–66.

Kawiana, I. G. P. (2023). Digital Leadership: Building Adaptive Organizations in The Digital Age. *Jurnal Multidisiplin Sahombu*, *3*(01), 170–179. DOI:10.58471/jms.v3i01.2709

Khurniawan, A. W., Irmawaty, & Supriadi, D. (2024). The impact of digital leadership on digital transformation in university organizations: an analysis of students' views. Perspectives of Science and Education, 67(1), 677–690. DOI:10.32744/pse.2024.1.38

Maulana Prawiro, W., & Rosi Subhiyakto, E. (2024). User-Centered Design Approaches to Enhance Employee Attendance Applications. *Advance Sustainable Science Engineering and Technology*, *6*(3), 02403025. DOI:10.26877/asset.v6i3.798

Ming, G. K., & Mansor, M. (2024). Unveiling Digital Leadership: Exploring Models and Theories. *South Asian Journal of Social Sciences and Humanities*, *5*(4), 1–17. DOI:10.48165/sajssh.2024.5401

Musaigwa, M. and Kalitanyi, V. (2023). Examining the leadership approaches adopted by fintech management when implementing organizational change prompted by digital transformation. Technology Audit and Production Reserves, 4(4(72)), 20–27. DOI:10.15587/2706-5448.2023.286627.

Ogbonna, E. (1992). Managing organisational culture: fantasy or reality?. Human resource Management journal, 3(2), 42–54.

Olafsen, A., Nilsen, E., Smedsrud, S., & Kamaric, D. (2020). Sustainable development through commitment to organizational change: the implications of organizational culture and individual readiness for change. Journal of Workplace Learning, ahead-of-print(ahead-of-print). DOI:10.1108/jwl-05-2020-0093

Peng, B. (2021). Digital leadership: State governance in the era of digital technology. *Cultures of Science*, *5*(4), 210–225. DOI:10.1177/2096608321989835

Pieretto, E., & Hinterhuber, A. (2021). *Digital transformation of manufacturing firms* (pp. 211–239). Routledge. DOI:10.4324/9781003008637-24

Salamzadeh, Y. (2024). Digital Leadership Competencies. In *Reference Module in Social Sciences*. Elsevier. DOI:10.1016/b978-0-443-13701-3.00156-0

Schein, E. H. (1992). Organizational culture and leadership. San Francisco: Jossey-Bass Inc.

Sheninger, E. (2019). Digital leadership: Changing paradigms for changing times. Corwin Press.

Solheim, M. and Skjølsvik, T. (2022). The impact of leadership on digital learning in health. European Conference on Knowledge Management, 23(2), 1106–1114. DOI:10.34190/eckm.23.2.648

Springs, D. (2024). Elements of Smart Leadership Approaches for Smart City Development. *Business Ethics and Leadership*, 8(2), 35–48. DOI:10.61093/bel.8(2).35-48.2024

2

The Impact of Digital Leadership on Organizational Innovation

Uncovering Self-Generated Innovation and Potential Opportunities

Erdal Kılıç[1] *& Memduh Begenirbaş*[2]

1. Introduction

In the contemporary era of swift digitization, the task of leadership becomes far more arduous and intricate compared to leading in an environment devoid of prospects or technical progress. Until the previous century, leadership was almost exclusively associated with physical strength and military intelligence. However, in the present day, leadership is scarcely linked to any form of physical power. As time progresses, it is evident that there will be no correlation between leadership and physical prowess. Amidst the fast proliferation of science and digitalization in the modern world, the resulting advancements and transformations have begun to complicate and question the aspects of leadership and management. Conducting a concurrent analysis of a substantial volume of data and addressing these components individually complicates a leader's role and amplifies their workload. Whether digital leadership has an effect on business success, innovative work behavior, and corporate innovation is the focus of this study. One factor that has led to the growing significance of digital leadership in recent times is the initiation or hastening of the digitalization process in several industries, namely

1 Lect, The National Defense University Army War School, <ekilic@kho.msu.edu.tr>
2 Prof. Dr., The National Defense University Army War School, <mbegenirbas@msu.edu.tr>

commencing in the early months of 2020 during the global Covid-19 outbreak. Throughout this process, remote working mechanisms have begun to be employed in the professional sphere, and the digital competencies of leaders have grown significantly more crucial. Limited study has been undertaken in the literature on digital leadership in corporate environments, with the majority of studies focused on elucidating the notion of digital leadership. The scarcity of research on the influence of digital leadership on innovative business behavior and corporate innovation suggests that this study will be advantageous to academic literature.

2. Essential Features of a Digital Leader

One of the most important duties that any leader should embrace in the modern era is the purpose of successfully leading enterprises forward in the digital era. To ensure that the business does not fall behind in terms of digital maturity, it is critical to understand and make the most of this change process. Furthermore, electricity drove this transition process during the industrial revolution a century ago. However, the current wave of change—which is occurring in a digital context and is happening much more quickly and thoroughly—has highlighted how crucial digital leadership is. Acknowledging that the digital environment is the site of this shift. (Ionology, 2020).

Leaders in the digital age, like their predecessors, must demonstrate more than just charisma, knowledge, and vision. In a globalizing world order where the breeze of competition is felt at every moment, and the economic and political conjuncture is constantly changing, the leaders of the new era must have many of the following characteristics: (Bennis,2013)

- Being future-oriented
- Having a vision
- Having the ability to encourage people
- Ability to detect and solve problems
- Have the ability to empathize
- Embracing the principle of ongoing education
- Create and demonstrate entrepreneurial spirit
- Acquire digital competencies

- Standard practices and methods, when deemed necessary, may be relinquished
- Maintain a robust professional network
- Actively utilize social media tools and intervene by learning about the negative aspects of your organization in a timely manner
- Maintaining the ability to adapt to rapid and continuous change

In order for a leader to be defined as a digital leader, he needs to have all three abilities at the same time. We can categorize these as possessing a digital mindset, digital skills, and the capacity to execute digital applications. (Hensellek,2020). This way, the digital leader can reliably formulate a digital vision and carry out digital transformation.

People who possess these features and equipment are believed to possess greater leadership potential in the digital age. Those who can adapt their attributes and behavior to the new age and who will take a step forward by developing their skills will be the most sought-after and preferred managers in the digital age.

Nowadays, when digital transformation is becoming imperative, many organizations need a leader with sufficient knowledge and skills to undertake the digitization process. Leadership is considered a key success factor for digital transformation that increases corporate success. (Proms, 2019).

3. Digital Leadership and Innovative Business Behavior

The staff's sense of security is psychologically influenced by their respect for leadership. An employee's emotional comfort and focus on their task result in a change in their working behavior. The personnel exhibiting innovative behavior demonstrates the emergence of novel ideas in a relaxed condition, free from tension, and experiencing a sense of spiritual solace. It is advisable for employees to embrace risk-taking and the possibility of failure in their commercial endeavors as a means of showcasing new approaches, all while maintaining close communication with their superiors. This scenario necessitates both interpersonal aptitude and psychological security. Confidence in a leader is an essential need for achieving psychological well-being. (Edmondson & Mogelof, 2006).

Digital leaders promote and encourage innovation within the organization. Digital leaders can positively influence market innovations. Leaders that possess a clear and compelling vision of innovation, along with self-assurance and a sense of authority, will make significant contributions to innovation in the marketplace. These executives foster a culture of innovation among their personnel to enable the successful implementation of new ideas and initiatives.

The significance of digitalization lies in its ability to proliferate globally, permeating all corners of the planet without being limited by spatial or temporal boundaries, much like the intricate network of blood vessels in the human body. Digitalization encompasses various aspects that are relevant to individuals, such as internet banking, e-government services, social networks, and wearable devices. The public sector significantly impacts inter-agency correspondence, e-government practices for citizens, and the digitization of consumer communication, marketing, product delivery, and business operations. Nevertheless, advancements and alterations in digital technologies present novel prospects and difficulties for both public and private organizations, as well as society at large. (Abbu, 2022). Neglecting to stay updated on emerging technologies in society results in disorder, destitution, and social unrest, while disregarding technological advancements in companies leads to closure and financial insolvency. (De Waal et al., 2016).

- Proficiency in Digital Leadership and Innovation

Digital leadership is crucial in fostering innovation. Digital leaders foster an organizational culture that encourages and facilitates the creation and execution of new ideas. This culture prioritizes the cultivation of employees' creativity and problem-solving abilities. Furthermore, digital leaders utilize digital platforms that foster cooperation and knowledge exchange to expedite the dissemination of information and generate synergies inside the organization. This enables businesses to acquire a competitive edge and enhance their market share. Digital leadership and innovation are essential and mutually reinforcing elements. (Guan, et al., 2003).

Digital leaders cultivate and solidify an innovative culture within their organizations. The strategic vision and technology expertise of digital leaders enable them to effectively oversee and execute innovation initiatives. For digital leaders to achieve their strategic goals and undergo digital transformation, innovation is critical. As digital leaders establish their organizations' future objectives, they incorporate their innovation processes into this overarching vision. Innovation is critical for digital leaders to achieve their goals, as it enables the development of creative ideas and strategies. This allows for adaptation to market changes and the acquisition of a competitive edge. (Wasono & Furinto, 2018).

Digital leadership and innovation are among the key factors determining success in today's world of business. With digital technologies evolving rapidly and ways of doing business changing, digital leaders have a critical role to play in increasing their organizations' competitiveness and continuously improving business performance. Its ability to innovate enables it to continuously innovate, adapt to changing market conditions, and achieve sustainable growth. The complementarity of these two concepts facilitates sustainable growth and enhances resilience to future uncertainties. Thus, those that develop digital leadership and innovation capabilities and integrate them into business processes have the potential to be more resilient and successful against the uncertainties of the future.

Leaders in the digital realm foster a climate of innovation within their organizations. Establishing a conducive workplace that fosters employees' inclination toward innovation, willingness to take calculated risks, and ability to generate imaginative solutions can be achieved. The capacity to innovate facilitates this cultural shift and allows for continuous innovation. Digital leaders reinforce this culture by leveraging digital platforms and tools to expedite information dissemination and improve collaboration. Digital leaders leverage the potential of technology to enhance corporate operations and create novel business frameworks. The capacity for innovation enables effective use of these technological capabilities and facilitates rapid adaptation to technological changes. This link improves organizations' operational efficiency and reduces costs (Tether & Tajar, 2008). In addition, digital transformation efforts can include a significant amount of uncertainty and danger. Competence in risk management is essential for digital leaders. In managing these risks and transforming uncertainties into opportunities, the capacity for innovation plays a crucial role. Innovation enhances the ability of businesses to withstand uncertainty and generates novel prospects.

4. The Interplay Between Digital Leadership and Innovative Business Behavior

One of the most prominent circumstantial factors that encourage employees to develop innovative business behaviors is leadership behavior (Huang, 2016). In this context, leadership behaviors play a crucial role in fostering an environment that motivates employees to adopt innovative business practices (Sethibe & Steyn, 2016). According to the theory of leader-member interaction, the communication between leaders and followers depends on the quality of communication and the result of communication (Graen et al., 1995). In this sense, we can think of a relationship-based type of leadership, based on mutual interactions, as important in shaping behavior. Transformational leadership and digital technologies combine to form digital leadership. (Waal et al., 2016). Digital leaders help organizations understand the changes that the digital age brings and quickly adapt to the process. These leaders look for opportunities for technology to work, understand how different stakeholders use technology to advance their own interests, and focus the organization on change, mobilizing all its resources toward that change. In addition, digital leaders support employees in improving their digital knowledge and skills (Wang et al., 2022).

- Originality and Creativity Define Entrepreneurial Behavior

One of the most fundamental characteristics of human structure is the desire to innovate. From the earliest days of human existence, the desire for survival and improvement has been a constant aspect of human behavior. In today's world, curiosity and tendency to challenge new formations are permeating a wider and wider sphere. One of the reasons for the increasing emphasis on innovation is that it can respond to demands in a much shorter time than the opportunities currently available.

Innovation is the transformation of knowledge into economic and social benefit. J. Schumpeter defines innovation in literature as the creation of a new element of production. According to Schumpeter, innovation involves work, such as discovering a new product, establishing a new production method, creating a new market, creating new resources to obtain semiconductors or raw materials, establishing monopoly markets, and so on in any industry (Schumpeter, 1997).

In order to be able to talk about innovative business behavior, the first thing staff want to do is to identify and measure every step of innovation work. Subsequently, the staff should be capable of identifying the problem, analyzing it, and pinpointing potential positive outcomes for the company that may result from the innovation. It is also necessary to examine examples of innovation that the employee is capable of implementing and then seek support to bring these ideas to life through their work and research, either within or outside the company. The final step in innovation is for the individual or company to produce a tangible product that embodies the idea or product they intend to develop (Carmeli et al., 2006).

5. Conclusion

In the present era of swiftly evolving technological advancements, digital transformation has become an unavoidable necessity. The crucial factor for organizations seeking successful digital transformation lies in the presence of leaders who can effectively implement and oversee the process of digital transition, rather than relying just on technology. The individual who will accomplish this task is the digital leader. A digital leader must possess a multitude of skills and abilities to fulfill this role. Central to this is a cognitive framework and a strategic outlook that will assist you in adopting and utilizing digital competencies. This allows the digital leader to efficiently carry out the required tasks during the development, execution, and oversight stages of digital transformation plans. Digital leaders have equal proficiency in both managerial and organizational skills, as well as digital skills.

Therefore, they have a significant impact on the development of digital transformation plans that are more successful, streamlined, and beneficial. In order to achieve a successful digital transformation, organizations need to empower their employees to align their efforts toward a common goal. This is the point at which the digital leader assumes responsibility. A digital leader may facilitate the adoption of digital transformation by setting a positive example, consistently acquiring new knowledge and skills, and maintaining open and honest communication. This will empower people at all levels of the organization to embrace digital leadership. In order to achieve success in the digital transformation process, organizations require digital leaders that can effectively oversee organizational change, accurately assess technological opportunities and dangers, and foster a digital culture that promotes ongoing learning.

Consequently, digital leadership, which has emerged as a modern form of leadership in recent times, can be considered as directing the path of the future. The transition to the digital era has a significant impact on every company function. Removal of barriers will improve this shift's chances of success. Possessing critical leadership abilities is required in order to be ready for this situation and to react promptly, while also transforming it into an institutional approach for the organization's ongoing operation. Advancements such as digital platforms, digital technologies, and tools, which continuously progress and update, are transforming organizations into a digital framework and emphasizing this in their operations. The digital leadership strategy has undergone changes because of factors such as the global COVID-19 pandemic. These developments have had an influence and increased the demand for digital leaders in the digital transformation process.

References

Abbu, H., Mugge, P., Gudergan, G., Hoeborn, G. ve Kwiatkowski, A. (2022). Measuring the Human Dimensions of Digital Leadership for Successful Digital Transformation. Research-Technology

Bennis, W. (2013). Leadership in a Digital World: Embracing Transparency and Adaptive Capacity, MIS Quarterly Vol. 37 No. 2/June 20. 635–637.

Carmeli, Abraham, Ravit Meitar ve Jacob Weisberg (2006). "Self-Leadership Skills and Innovative Behavior at Work." International Journal of Manpower

De Waal, B., Outvorst, F. ve Ravesteyn, P. (2016). Digital Leadership: The Objective-Subjective Dichotomy of Technology Revisited. Proceedings of the Conference on European Management Leadership

Edmondson AC, Mogelof JP. (2006). Explaining psychological safety in innovation teams: Organizational culture, team dynamics, or personality

Guan, J., & Ma, N. (2003). Innovative capability and export performance of Chinese firms. Technovation, 23(9), 737–747. DOI:10.1016/S0166-4972(02)00013-5

Hensellek, S. (2020). Digital leadership: A framework for successful leadership in the digital age. Journal of Media Management and Entrepreneurship (JMME), 2(1), 55-69.

Howells, J., Tether, B., Gallouj, F., Djellal, F., Gallouj, C., Blind, K., ... & Banach, D. (2004). *Innovation in Services: Issues at Stake and Trends* (Doctoral dissertation, European Commission).

Ionology. (2020). The World's Most Practical Digital Transformation Courses. <https://www.ionology.com/>

Promsri, C. (2019). The developing model of digital leadership for a successful digital transformation. GPH-International Journal of Business Management (IJBM), 2(08), 01–08.

Schumpeter, J. A. (1997), Theorie der Wirtschaftlichen Entwicklung: Eine Untersuchung über Unternehmergewinn, Kapital, Kredit, Zins und den Konjunkturzyklus, Duncker & Humblot, Berlin.

Wasono, L. W., & Furinto, A. (2018). The effect of digital leadership and innovation management for incumbent telecommunication company in the digital disruptive era. International Journal of Engineering & Technology,

3

The Role of Digital Leadership in Improving Employee Performance and Business Success

Kemal Eroğluer[1]

1. Introduction

Human beings have to live together with other people by nature. This requires people to live in communities where specific rules and regulations prevail. Since the early times of history, people's ability to live in organized communities and achieve their goals has been enabled by leaders with different characteristics and abilities than others.

In today's world where great changes are taking place, technology creates significant effects in every aspect of life. Technology, which offers many opportunities that make people's lives easier, has recently significantly changed the habits and expectations of people and societies with digitalization. This change requires leaders who will guide people, groups and society, who are constantly exposed to the effects of the digitalizing world, to have digital culture, talent and philosophy. In order to ensure the performance and success of employees in the digitalizing business world, leaders should act by combining basic leadership qualities as well as the qualities required by the digital age with modern managerial practices (Hensellek, 2020, p. 55).

2. Conceptual Framework

Leadership and Digital Leadership

Leadership, which is the basic element of the management process, has emerged as a natural consequence of the necessity of people living together (Güney, 2021, p. 1).

1 Assoc. Prof., The National Defense University Army War School <k_erogluer@yahoo.com.tr>

Leadership: it is expressed as a process consisting of the leader, the managed and the conditions (Koçel, 2014). Leader is "the sum of knowledge and abilities aimed at gathering a group of people around certain goals and mobilizing them to achieve these goals" (Bakan et al., 2013, p. 72), in another definition, it is stated as "a person who motivates others to act for a certain purpose, inspires and influences them, and makes those people follow her/him willingly" (Koçel, 2014). Leadership is seen as a "strategic process" (Fry, 2003, p. 694) that helps develop the potential of employees and guides (Sürücü, 2021, p. 225). Cultural change and integration experienced under the influence of globalization, employee mobility and diversity, developments in information and communication technologies and digitalization, as well as new regulations in business life, have brought about new leadership approaches (Antonakis and Day, 2017).

The digitalization process experienced with the developments in information technologies and the invention of the internet has affected all areas of life. In this process, the phenomenon of constant change has become a way of life. These changes and developments also had an impact on leaders and forced them to create new management styles and strategies. Leaders who embrace the necessity of digital culture and technological applications in the digital age and can develop future strategies accordingly will lead organizations to success. Leaders with this culture and competence are seen as digital leaders.

Digitalization requires technical skills to deal with and understand digital technologies, as well as a digital mindset; so that decision-makers can recognize and properly evaluate the opportunities and challenges associated with digitalization (Hensellek, 2020, p. 55). Technology leadership and transformational leadership are prerequisites in the definition of digital leadership, which must have a digital mindset (Büyükbeşe and Doğan, 2022, p. 174).

Digital leadership has been defined as "a type of leadership that can effectively use the management, business and strategic thinking skills of different disciplines with the help of the tools offered by the digital age" (Şahin et al., 2020, p. 272–273). A digital leader is defined as a leader who improves communication in the organization and has the power to influence individuals, groups and organizations in the use of information (Horney et al., 2010, p. 33; Mert, 2024, p. 38). Digital leadership is not a leadership style that can be explained by competencies and abilities executed in only one field. Because of that reason digital leadership should not be limited to the use of technology alone. Since leadership requires a multi-dimensional perspective, they must be able to synthesize issues such as strategy, culture, communication, human relations and success along with technology and open up new horizons to their followers.

Digital leaders must be agents of change. Digital leaders are individuals who can take risks, are talented, can learn from the consequences of risks, and can manage change within the organization and themselves (Örücü and Hasırcı, 2024, p. 13). In addition, qualities such as "agility, adaptation and being a pioneer in rapid change" are among the characteristics expected from digital leaders (Güler, 2023, p.12). Digital leaders must have superior communication skills, be able to develop and implement strategies, be open-minded, be able to quickly adapt to innovations, and be able to use technology well (isbank.com.tr/blog/dijital- donusum). Digital leaders are leaders who are people-oriented, attach importance to cooperation and trust among employees, have organizational skills, can create new models, work with individuals through new and different perspectives, and can adapt their organizations to changes through different technologies. At the same time, digital leaders should be able to harmonize digital tools with the organizational structure (Örücü and Hasırcı, 2024, p.14).

Employee Performance and Business Success

Performance is expressed as "the success shown in performing any work, play or business; achievement" (www.tdk.gov.tr), "level of work fulfillment" (Çelik et al., 2022, p. 565). Performance from an institutional perspective; "The percentage of the organization achieving its goals or objectives by looking at the results of the work done in a certain period of time" (Yardım, 2024, p. 48), Employee performance is defined as follows (Uğurlu and Köksal, 2022, p. 287) "a product of talent and motivation used to motivate employees to get the best out of themselves" (Moorhead and Griffin, 1998). It is a concept that expresses how successful an individual is while performing the set of tasks that constitute his/her job and to what extent he/she can fulfill the requirements of his/her job (Baş and Artar, 1990, p. 13). Performance is the ability of an employee to take on tasks and responsibilities in a business to meet their needs and spend time and effort to get what they want (Barutçugil, 2002, p. 40).

Performance, which is among the main determining factors of success in business life, is related to people. Employees who are the main members of the organization also dedicate their life for its survival and success. There is a relationship based on mutuality between employees and organizations. Organizations try to achieve their goals through the talents, education levels, labor, and efforts of employees. Employees also expect to gain benefits and morale due to the organizational activities they perform. The increased effort from the point where mutual expectations meet is considered as the employee's positive performance.

Many factors affect the performance of employees. These factors have generally been evaluated in three different areas: personal factors including demographic characteristics and the individual's abilities and responsibilities, organizational factors related to the system and management, and environmental factors consisting of the internal and external environment (Maden, 2019, p. 58). Despite all the possibilities and opportunities to motivate a person with a complex emotional structure and increase her performance, he/she may often need the magic touch of a leader. The behaviors of leaders who exhibit supportive approaches can have an impact on the performance of employees.

Employee performance has been examined in two dimensions: task performance and contextual performance. Task performance refers to the technical skills employees have for the job. At the same time, technical skills create task performance of lower-level employees. Another element of task performance is managerial performance, which refers to the direction and guidance of upper-level employees to lower-level employees. Contextual performance deals with the social dimension of working life (Yardım, 2024, p. 49). While task performance, which constitutes the dimension of performance, is related to job-specific abilities and formal job description, contextual performance is related to all jobs, motivation and personality, as well as extra-role behavior (Riketta, 2002; Sonnentag et al., 2008; Topcuoğlu et al., 2024, p.25).

Success, which constitutes one step of Maslow's hierarchy of needs, is one of the basic motivational elements of humans and is defined as "success" and "work performance" (www.tdk.gov.tr). It can be thought that the concept of success is among the instinctive motives of humans. Since success is a basic source of motivation, it affects both the psychological and physical health of the individual.

Today, organizations expect employees to contribute more and consider employees who achieve this as successful. Employees' job success is affected by a number of factors.

These factors are listed as personal factors, organizational factors, environmental factors, psychological factors, psycho-social factors, employee needs, motivation and stress and social qualities (Gültekin, 2009, p. 51–131; Baysal, 2020, p. 48–93).

Leaders are very important for open system organizations to achieve success in the digital age. Leaders must create and implement strategies to achieve their goals by carefully evaluating the strengths and weaknesses of the organization, as well as the opportunities and threats presented by the external environment. Making the opportunities provided by technology effectively available to employees can positively affect their performance and business success.

Digital leaders can take advantage of interactive training that is among the opportunities offered by digitalization. They can contribute to the personal development of employees with such training (Anwar and Saraih, 2024). With the help of information systems, they can measure and control the contribution of these training courses to the performance of employees. Personal development of employees with digitalization can increase competition among them.

With the use of digital technologies, working hours can be made flexible to meet the needs of employees. By arranging working hours, employees' motivation can be increased by making positive contributions to their work-life balance.

An information architecture can be established that will provide quick access to the procedures and instructions needed to use new technologies. With this information architecture, digital leaders can manage business processes more consciously and increase the effectiveness and efficiency of their employees.

With the use of mobile applications and the internet, which are communication opportunities offered by digitalization, communication within the organization can be made more horizontal and communication between employees can be strengthened. This can lead to the emergence of a structure that understands and supports each other better.

With the help of opportunities such as virtual training, simulation and modeling offered by technology, digital leaders create learning organizations and encourage learning for each employee, contributing to the development of the organization's business processes. The learning organization climate created will increase the quality of the organization's goods and services and will also provide significant gains for its stakeholders.

With the help of digital applications, employees' abilities can be determined more accurately, and task distribution and responsibility sharing can be done more appropriately. Continuously updating job descriptions and ensuring the specialization of employees accordingly, especially by enabling the use of opportunities such as artificial intelligence, are important contributions that digital leaders can make to organizations. The transfer of the opportunities offered by the digital world to organizational processes by leaders can, on the one hand, create positive effects on the abilities of employees, and on the other hand, increase the competitive power of organizations by increasing their opportunities and capabilities.

Although the basic factors affecting the business success of employees in today's digital world are similar, it is inevitable to see the effects of digital transformation. Leaders play an important role in this process. It is evaluated that the business success of employees who use the opportunities offered by technology will be positively affected if leaders with digital culture support and guide their employees. It can be stated that the psychological well-being of employees has positive effects on their performance (Uslu and Şimşek, 2020, p. 6).

3. Conclusion

In order to gain competitive advantage and be successful in the digital age, businesses must constantly adjust their business processes, product and service offerings according to changing customer demands and expectations. This process, which constitutes the first stage of digital transformation, is seen to reorganize the business world with the development of e-commerce, the widespread use of social media and the development of cloud computing (Mert, 2024, p. 2).

Digital leaders must create digital reality and digital desire in their organization and business processes. The digital capacity of the business should be established based on its future forecasts and strategies. The digitalization process should be continued in a cycle with digital adaptation and digital applications (Yağcı, 2023, p. 29). Nowadays, for leaders to be successful, it has become a necessity to synthesize the requirements of digitalization with the strategies they have determined during the digital transformation phase (Alan and Köker, 2021, p. 248).

A digital leader is considered a leader who has a risk-taking culture, is flexible, can cooperate with customers and employees, adopts transformative strategies, and is open to innovation (Sow and Aborbie, 2018). Digital leaders empowering their employees regarding organizational activities to be carried out in the digital world and ensuring their participation in decision-making processes can increase the performance and business success of employees.

References

Alan, H. ve Köker, A. R. (2021). Stratejik Liderlikten Dijital Stratejik Liderliğe: Kavramsal ve Kuramsal Bir Tartışma. Türkiye Siyaset Bilimi Dergisi. 4(2), 235–252.

Antonakis, J. ve Day, D. V. (2017). The Nature of Leadership. 3rd Edition, SAGE Publications.

Anwar, S. and Saraih, U. N. (2024). "Digital leadership in the digital era of education: enhancing knowledge sharing and emotional intelligence," International Journal of Educational Management, Vol. ahead-of-print No. ahead-of-print. DOI:10.1108/IJEM-11-2023-0540 Bakan, İ., Büyükbeşe, T., Erşahan, B., ve Kefe, İ. (2013). Kadın çalışanların yöneticilere ilişkin algıları: Bir alan çalışması. Çankırı Karatekin Üniversitesi İktisadi ve İdari Bilimler Fakültesi Dergisi, 3, 71–84.

Barutçugil, İ. (2002). Performans Yönetimi, Kariyer Yayıncılık İletişim Eğitim Hizmetleri Ltd. Şti., İstanbul.

Baş, İ. M. ve Artar, A. (1990). İşletmelerde Verimlilik Denetimi, MPM Yayıncılık, Ankara.

Baysal, A. (2020). Sendikaların İşçi ve İşveren İlişkileri Üzerindeki Rolünün Türkiye'de Sendika Yöneticilerinin İş Başarısına ve Sendikal Bağlılığa Etkisi: Metal İşkolunda Bir Araştırma. Yüksek Lisans Tezi. İstanbul Aydın Üniversitesi. İstanbul.

Büyükbeşe, T. ve Doğan, Ö. (2022). Dijital Liderliğin Yenilikçi İş Davranışı ve İş Performansı Üzerine Etkisi. Akademik Araştırmalar ve Çalışmalar Dergisi, 14(26), 173–186.

Çelik, S., Bozkurt Çetinkaya, Ö. ve Ekşili, N. (2022). Çalışan Performansı Ölçeğindeki İfadelerin Karar Ağacı Algoritması İle Belirlenmesi Mehmet Akif Ersoy İktisadi ve İdari Bilimler Fakültesi Dergisi, 9(1): 561–584.

Fry, L. W. (2003). Toward a Theory of Spiritual Leadership. The Leadership Quarterly, 14(6), 693–727.

Güler, H. N. (2023). Dijital Liderlik Çalışmalarının Analizi. Topkapı Journal of Social Science, 2(2), 11–19.

Güney, S. (2021). Lider ve Liderlik. 1. Bölüm Dünden Bugüne Liderlik İçinde. Ed. Semra Güney. Nobel Akademik Yayıncılık. Ankara

Gürüz, D. ve Gürel, E. (2006). Yönetim ve Organizasyon. Ankara: Nobel Yayıncılık.

Hensellek, S. (2020). Digital Leadership: A Framework for Successful Leadership in the Digital Age. Journal of Media Management and Entrepreneurship, 2(1): 55–69.

Horney, N., Passmore, B. ve O'shea, T. (2010). Leadership Agility: A Business Imperative for a VUCA World. People & Strategy, 33(4), 32–38.

Koçel, T. (2014). İşletme Yöneticiliği: Yönetim ve Organizasyon, Organizasyonlarda Davranış, Klasik-Modern-Çağdaş ve Güncel Yaklaşımlar. İstanbul: Beta Yayınevi.

Maden, F. M. (2019). Toxic Workplaces, Toxic Leaders and Effect on Organizational Commitment and Employee Performance. Master's Thesis, Bahçeşehir University Social Sciences Institute MBA Program. Istanbul.

Mert, M. (2024). Dijital Liderlik ve Örgütsel Çeviklik İlişkisi Üzerine Bir Araştırma. Doktora Tezi. Pamukkale Üniversitesi Sosyal Bilimler Enstitüsü. Denizli.

Moorhead, G. ve Grıffın, R. W. (1989). Organizational Behavior, Houghton and Mifflin Comp., 2. Edition.

Örücü, E. ve Hasırcı, I. (2024). Dijital liderlik ve kapsayıcı liderliğin çalışanların dijital yetenekleri üzerindeki etkisi: Bankacılık sektörü üzerine bir araştırma. KOCATEPEİİBFD, 26(1), 136–151.

Riketta, M. (2002). Attitudinal organizational commitment and job performance: A meta-analysis. Journal of Organizational Behavior, 23(3), 257–266.

Sonnentag, S., Volmer, J. ve Spychala, A. (2008). The SAGE handbook of organizational behavior: Volume I–Micro Approaches. In The SAGE Handbook of Organizational Behavior: Volume I–Micro Approaches (pp. 427–448).

Sow, M. ve Aborbie, S. (2018). Impact of leadership on digital transformation. Business and Economic Research, 8(3), 139–148

Sürücü, L. (2021). Liderlik Tarzlarının Çalışan Performansına Etkisinde İş Tatminin Aracı Rolü. S. 223- 238. Ed. Prof. Dr. Mahmut Yardımcıoğlu. Sosyal, Beşeri ve İdari Bilimler Alanında Uluslararası Araştırmalar V, Eğitim Yayınevi, Konya.

Şahin, Ç. Ç., Avcı, Y. E., ve Sabri, A. N. I. K. (2020). Dijital liderlik algısının metaforlar yoluyla incelenmesi. Elektronik Sosyal Bilimler Dergisi, 19(73), 271–328.

Topcuoğlu,E., Kobanoğlu, M. S., Kaygın, E. Karafakioğlu, E., Uygungil Erdoğan, S., Turan Torun, B. ve Oktaysoy, O. (2023). The Improving Role of Digital Leadership in the Impact of Social Loafing on Job Performance. International Journal of Organizational Leadership 12(1): 22–40.

Uğurlu, A. ve Köksal, K. (2022). Bağlılık, Çalışan Performansı ve İş Tatmini İlişkisinde Özgeciliğin Düzenleyici Rolü: Sağlık Çalışanları Üzerinde Bir Uygulama, İşletme Araştırmaları Dergisi, 14 (1), 284–302.

Uslu, O. ve Şimşek, A. (2020). Çalışma arkadaşlarına güven ve psikolojik iyi oluşun çalışanların iş performansına etkileri. Sakarya Üniversitesi İşletme Enstitüsü Dergisi. 2(1), 6–12.

Yağcı, M. (2023). İşletmelerde Dijital Dönüşümün Finansal Performansa Etkisi: Kobilerde Bir Araştırma. Yüksek Lisans Tezi. Aydın Adnan Menderes Üniversitesi Sosyal Bilimler Enstitüsü. Aydın.

Yardım, A. (2024). Ödüllendirme Sistemlerinin Örgütsel Bağlılık ve Çalışan Performansına Etkisi: Beyaz Yaka Çalışanlar Üzerine Bir Uygulama. Yüksek Lisans Tezi. Kayseri Üniversitesi Lisansüstü Eğitim Enstitüsü. Kayseri.
<https://sozluk.gov.tr/İsbank.com.tr/blog/dijital-donusum>

4

Digital Transformation Business Strategies and Leadership in the Digital Age

Brave Ideas for a Brave New World

Onur Oktaysoy[1] *& Akif Yenikaya*[2]

1. Introduction

The digital age has brought about a radical transformation in the business world with rapidly changing technology and information flow. This transformation has profoundly affected not only business processes but also leadership approaches, business models and strategic processes of businesses. The effects of digital transformation have reshaped the ability of businesses to gain competitive advantage and ensure their sustainability. Digital transformation, which has become an inevitable reality in the business world, offers businesses the opportunity to become more efficient, flexible and customer-oriented by adopting digital technologies. In this process, understanding the basic components of digital transformation is critical for developing and implementing a successful strategy. In this context, it is a necessity to find answers to questions such as what digital transformation is, how, where and when it will be realized, what it will affect, how it will affect, why it should be realized and, perhaps most importantly, who will carry out all these. At this point, the management of the transformation process is at the focus of these problems, where the answers may differ according to each organization, the sector in which the organization in question is located, and even whether the organization is multinational or national scale. Accordingly, in this section, it is aimed to draw a framework about the digital transformation process, to define digital leadership, which can be defined as a relatively new

1 Asst. Prof., Kafkas University, <onuroktaysoy@kafkas.edu.tr>
2 Asst. Prof., Kafkas University, <akifyenikaya@kafkas.edu.tr>

concept in the context of the management of the transformation process in question, and to determine the qualities that should be found in the leader for the successful realization of the digital transformation process. This study, which includes examples of multinational organizations that have managed to adapt to the requirements of the digital age and successfully continue the transformation process and examples of digital leaders who have led these organizations to success, aims to provide a different perspective on the concepts of digital transformation and digital leadership, and to provide readers with practical information and inspiring examples of how they can develop digital transformation strategies in their own sectors.

2. Definition and Importance of Digital Transformation

2.1. What is Digital Transformation?

Digital transformation is a comprehensive process in which businesses restructure the way they do business and customer interactions using digital technologies. This process aims to increase efficiency, reduce costs, and maximize customer satisfaction through digital tools and platforms.

Digital transformation, which can be defined as a comprehensive concept describing the transformative impact of technology on the business world and social structures, generally refers to the radical change in the way businesses and organizations do business through the use of digital technologies. This transformation process involves not only the integration of technological tools but also the restructuring of business models, operational processes, customer experiences, organizational culture and values. While digital transformation redefines the dynamics of the business world, it enables businesses to be more efficient, competitive, and customer-oriented (Gebayew et al., 2018).

Digital transformation is a comprehensive and complex process that starts with the awareness that the current state of an organization is insufficient to meet its expectations and develops with the organization's will to transform. (Westerman & Bonnet, 2015). This process, which involves adopting digital technologies and reshaping business processes, models, and strategies, is usually carried out in four stages: awareness, realization, transformation, and continuous innovation (Deloitte, 2015).

2.2. Importance of Digital Transformation

Digital transformation is critical for businesses to gain competitive advantage, increase operational efficiency, and maximize customer satisfaction. The main benefits of digital transformation for businesses are as follows:

Competitive Advantage: Businesses that use digital technologies effectively can act faster and more flexibly than their competitors. Digital technologies allow businesses to quickly analyze large amounts of data and make faster decisions with insights derived from this data. This increases the ability of businesses to respond faster to changes in the market and customer expectations (Hussain et al., 2023).

Cost Savings: Digital transformation increases efficiency by significantly reducing operational costs. Digital technologies enable the automation of business processes, reducing human errors and minimizing operational costs; Internet of things (IoT) devices enable the optimization of inventory and logistics processes; and cloud computing technologies enable businesses to reduce information technologies (IT) costs and provide scalability.

Innovation: Digital transformation has an important place for businesses in terms of encouraging the development of innovative business models and products. Digital technologies accelerate research and development processes, enabling innovative products and services to be launched faster. Big data analytics and artificial intelligence can be used to better understand customer needs and market trends. In addition, digital tools and 3D printers accelerate product development processes, enabling rapid prototyping and testing of ideas (Shehadeh et al., 2023).

Customer Satisfaction: Digital technologies make it possible to offer customers a consistent and integrated experience through various channels (web, mobile, social media, etc.). Thanks to digital technologies such as artificial intelligence and chatbots, customer service and support processes can be improved, and customers' questions can be answered quickly and effectively. In addition, with the qualified business structures created with digital transformation, it becomes possible to collect and analyze customer data, thus better understanding the needs and preferences of customers. While this information opens up space for businesses to offer the right marketing campaigns and personalized services, it can also positively affect their ability to compete.

Data-Driven Decisions: Data-driven decision making can be defined as an approach where decisions are supported by data and analytical methods. Data-driven decisions are based on a different understanding than traditional decision-making processes based on intuition or experience. Decisions made with these methods enable businesses to act on objective data and analyses, so that more accurate and precise inferences can be made. Data-driven decision-making processes, one of the most important components of digital transformation, are highly functional in terms of enabling organizations to minimize risks and gain competitive advantage while increasing their performance.

Why Has Digital Transformation Become So Important?

Digital transformation has become a major focus of interest in academic, industrial and public areas in recent years. Rapid advances in information and communication technologies, competitive pressures brought about by globalization and increasing expectations of customers have made digital transformation an inevitable process. Digital transformation is not only a technological innovation but also a strategic necessity. The benefits it provides in many areas such as competitive advantage, customer experience, operational efficiency, data management and flexibility increase the importance of digital transformation day by day. Academic literature and current practices show that digital transformation is an inevitable process for organizations and companies that do not adapt to this process will face the risk of losing their competitive advantage. Therefore, the development and implementation of digital transformation strategies should be seen as one of the keys to success in today's business world (Hussain et al., 2023).

One of the most significant areas of differentiation brought about by technology-induced changing conditions is undoubtedly economic structures. Adapting to this new economic system, in which the dynamics between the business and the customer have radically changed, has become a matter of existence and non-existence for businesses. These trends are categorized under twelve headings in the literature (Kurpayanidi, 2023). These are

- ***Information*:** Economization of information (smart clothes, smart cars, smart TVs, smart phones, etc.).

- *Digitalization*: The penetration of digital economy into all areas of life (public, finance, health, etc.).
- *Virtual World*: Virtualization of traditional physical structures (virtual company, virtual bank, virtual health etc.).
- *Molecularization*: Molecular economy (fragmentation of old company structures).
- *Integration/Networking*: The disappearance of physical borders, cyber connectivity.
- *Disintermediation*: Elimination of intermediaries between producers and consumers through digital means.
- *Meeting at a Point*: Bringing different sectors together, equal opportunities, market balance.
- *Innovation*: Expectation of innovation and innovation in every field.
- *Producer-Consumer*: Blurring the distance between producer and consumer.
- *Urgency*: The urgent need for speed in every field.
- *Globalization*: Global economy and the transformation of sociology.
- *Conflict*: Conflict caused by changing conditions, expectation-value change, dominance of uncertainty.

These trends listed above affect not only businesses and economic systems, but also every field whose subject is human, thus making digital transformation important.

3. Opportunities and Challenges of Digital Age

The digital age has been shaped by rapid developments in information and communication technologies and has led to radical changes in almost every aspect of society. The opportunities and challenges of this era play an important role in determining the digital transformation strategies of individuals, businesses and governments (Bharadwaj et al., 2013). One of the most obvious opportunities of the digital age is the ease of access to information. Thanks to the Internet and mobile technologies, people can access information instantly from anywhere in the world. This provides great advantages in many areas such as education, health, research and business (Chen et al., 2012). Another important opportunity is that businesses become more efficient and flexible with digital technologies. Technologies such as automation, artificial intelligence and big data analytics enable businesses to optimize their operational processes, reduce costs and increase customer satisfaction (Brynjolfsson & McAfee, 2014). The digital age also creates new business models and entrepreneurial opportunities. Digital platforms enable innovative business ideas to be realized and entrepreneurs to operate globally. For example, sharing economy models have revolutionized traditional sectors with platforms such as Airbnb and Uber (Verhoef et al., 2019).

However, these opportunities brought by the digital age come with various challenges. Foremost among these are cyber security risks. With increasing digitalization, the number of cyber-attacks and data breaches is also increasing. This situation requires individuals and businesses to be more careful in protecting their personal and commercial information. In particular, critical infrastructures and financial systems are becoming more vulnerable to cyber threats (Davenport & Ronanki, 2018). Another important challenge is the existence of the digital divide. Inequalities in access to and use of digital technologies create significant differences between individuals and societies. While people and businesses in developed countries can benefit more from the opportunities offered by digital transformation, many people and businesses in developing countries are deprived of these opportunities (Bharadwaj et al., 2013). Another distinct challenge brought by the digital age is concerns about privacy and data protection. Digital platforms and applications collect and process large amounts of personal data of users. The lack of transparency about how this data is used and protected increases users' privacy concerns. Although legal regulations such as the General Data Protection Regulation (GDPR) have taken steps to address these concerns, there are still significant gaps in data protection (Porter & Heppelmann, 2015). In addition to all this, the rapid change brought about by the digital age is leading to a major transformation in the labor market. Automation and artificial intelligence cause some jobs to disappear and the demand for new skills to increase. This situation requires employees to constantly update themselves and acquire new skills. However, this transition process may lead to uncertainties and social problems in the labor market (Brynjolfsson & McAfee, 2014).

4. Leadership in the Digital Age

The digital age is a period in which technology is advancing rapidly and access to and sharing of information is easier than ever. Leadership in this era requires going beyond traditional approaches and developing new strategies and skills in line with the requirements of digital transformation. The changes brought about by the digital age emphasize leaders' adaptability, openness to innovation, farsightedness, and digital competencies (Oktaysoy et al., 2023). At this point, the digital leadership approach gains importance as the leadership model of the digital age. Digital leadership is defined as "a leadership style that can fulfill the roles attributed to the leader in the digital age by making use of digital tools, mastering digital technologies, and managing the organisation" (Topcuoğlu et al., 2023). Pearl Zhu (2015) defines digital leadership as a combination of five different leadership approaches: thought leadership, creative leadership, visionary leadership, curious leadership, and wise leadership.

Leaders in the digital age need to have a number of qualities different from traditional leaders. Some of these qualities can be listed as follows:

***Innovation and Technology Orientation*:** Leadership in the digital age requires the ability to think innovatively and master technology. Innovation involves not only improving existing processes, but also the capacity to create radical changes and new business models. Digital leaders closely follow technological developments and gain competitive advantage by integrating these technologies into business processes.

***Flexibility and Rapid Adaptation*:** Digital transformation requires businesses to adapt to rapidly changing market conditions and customer expectations. In this context, digital leaders should have flexible and fast adaptation skills. In times of crisis and uncertainty, they can develop flexible strategies and guide their organizations by making quick decisions.

***Foresight and Strategic Thinking*:** Leadership in the digital age requires foresight and strategic thinking. Digital leaders anticipate future trends and opportunities and position their organizations accordingly. In this context, setting long-term vision and strategic goals is of great importance for digital age leadership.

Human-Centered Approach and Cultural Transformation: Even in a technology-driven world, the human factor is still the key to success. Digital leaders aim to maximize the talents and potential of their employees by adopting a people-oriented approach. Increasing employee motivation, supporting talent development and creating an inclusive work culture are the focal elements of leadership in the digital age.

Data-Driven Decision Making: As mentioned before, data-driven decision making has an important place in the digital age leadership approach. Technologies such as big data analytics and artificial intelligence enable leaders to make more informed and accurate decisions, thus contributing to the continuous monitoring and analysis of business processes and organizational performance and thus improving the management process. In this way, it is possible to gain a competitive advantage and achieve sustainable success.

Collaboration and Networking: Digital transformation has increased the importance of collaboration and networking. Digital leaders develop innovative solutions by collaborating not only within their own organizations but also with external stakeholders. These collaborations can create value in a wide range of areas from supply chain management to customer relations. In addition, digital leaders use their global networks to integrate best practices and innovations into their organizations, thereby contributing to a sustainable competitive advantage for their organizations.

5. Examples of Digital Leaders from Today's World

Satya Nadella — CEO of Microsoft: Satya Nadella became CEO of Microsoft in 2014 and completely changed the strategic direction of the company, tripling its market capitalization. Nadella redefined Microsoft with a focus on *cloud computing and artificial intelligence* and made the Azure platform a global leader in its field.

Nevzat Aydın—Founder and CEO of Yemeksepeti: Aydın founded Yemeksepeti and revolutionized the e-commerce sector in Turkey. The company achieved great success in online food ordering and was acquired by Delivery Hero in 2015. Nevzat Aydın has been an important role model in the digital entrepreneurship ecosystem with Yemeksepeti and contributed to the development of the *digital entrepreneurship* ecosystem in Turkey.

Jeff Bezos—Amazon Founder and Former CEO: By founding Amazon, Jeff Bezos has revolutionized the *e-commerce and logistics* industry with global impact. With its customer-oriented approach and logistics excellence, Amazon has become a pioneer in the sector in which it operates and has succeeded in taking the competition to a different dimension. Not only limited to e-commerce, but Bezos also entered the cloud computing market with Amazon Web Services (AWS) and provided leadership in this field.

Elon Musk—CEO of Tesla and SpaceX: Elon Musk has revolutionized the automotive industry with Tesla and the space industry with SpaceX. Musk has become an important leader that comes to mind when it comes to technology, innovation and digital transformation, while ensuring the widespread use of *electric-autonomous vehicles* with Tesla and making significant innovations in space transport with SpaceX.

Murat Erkan—Turkcell CEO: Mr. Erkan played an important role in Turkcell's digital transformation process. He expanded the company's digital services and enriched the customer experience with products such as Lifecell, BiP, TV+, fizy and Dergilik, while also investing in innovative areas such as *5G technology and IoT*, making Turkcell a technology leader.

Reed Hastings—CEO of Netflix: Reed Hastings is one of the most important examples of a digital leader who transformed Netflix from a DVD rental company into one of the world's largest digital content platforms. By embracing *digital streaming technology* and investing in original content production, Hastings has helped Netflix become a global brand.

Eren Bali—Udemy Founder and CEO of Carbon Health: Bali has taken bold steps in the *digital transformation* of traditional services and created a worldwide platform in the online education sector by founding Udemy. After that, he founded Carbon Health, a healthcare technology startup, and made a significant contribution to the digital transformation of healthcare services.

6. Digital Strategies and Business Models

Digital strategies refer to the process of integrating digital technologies into the business processes of businesses and using these technologies in line with the overall strategic goals of the business (Bharadwaj et al., 2013). Successful implementation of digital strategies, which are developed to provide businesses with competitive advantage, increase customer satisfaction and optimize operational efficiency, enables businesses to adapt to dynamic market conditions quickly and effectively (Porter & Heppelmann, 2015). Digital business models can be conceptualized as new and innovative ways of doing business created by integrating digital technologies into business processes. These models redefine the value creation, value delivery and value capture processes of businesses (Teece, 2010). The transformation process of digital business models generally consists of the following stages:

Analyzing the Current Business Model: At this stage, the business model currently used by the business and its digital competences are evaluated in the context of the goals and objectives of the business, market conditions and perceived competitive intensity (Zhang et al., 2015).

Digital Strategy Development: If, as a result of the analysis of the current business model, there is a conviction that the business needs to carry out a digital transformation, strategic goals and a roadmap to be followed are determined for the desired transformation (Blaschke et al., 2017).

Implementation and Integration: At this stage, the strategies developed for digital transformation are implemented and the necessary digital technologies are integrated into business processes (Rachinger et al., 2019).

Performance Measurement and Continuous Improvement: In the measurement and improvement phase, which is the last phase, the effects of the transformation carried out by the enterprise are measured and evaluated from the expected strategy-actualized strategy axis, and strategies are updated according to the results obtained (Oktaysoy et al. 2023).

Digital business models are at the center of digital transformation and are critical for businesses to gain competitive advantage. Digital business models, in which the effective use of digital technologies, the development of innovative business models and customer-oriented strategies are at the forefront, can be implemented in various ways in different sectors. Some of these applications are as follows:

E-commerce: It is a digital business model that enables trading over the Internet and includes many commercial activities such as the sale of products and services, receiving payments and managing customer relations (Olifirov et al., 2019).

Subscription Models: Subscription-based business models for digital content and services. Subscription models stand out as a strong business model that provides sustainable growth and competitive advantage in the digital business world (Mihova & Chukalov, 2019).

Platform Economy: This business model is based on the idea of bringing together different user groups through digital platforms and facilitating their interaction. The platform economy business model is a common business model that uses digital technologies to optimize the processes of creating, distributing and capturing economic value (Shpylyk et al., 2021).

Freemium Models: Freemium business models are business models that allow users to use the basic features of the services subject to value for free, while charging for premium features (Seufert, 2013).

Data-Driven Models: Data-driven models are business models that transform data into an economy by using it as a core value, optimize business processes, develop new products and services, and provide competitive advantages (Zolnowski et al., 2017).

Sharing Economy Models: Sharing economy model is a comprehensive business model concept that includes economic models based on the sharing or joint use of goods and services (Ritter & Schanz, 2019).

7. Conclusion

In this section, it is aimed to draw a framework about the importance of integrating digital transformation into business strategies, while also trying to detail the critical role played by leaders in this process. Rapid adoption of technological innovations, enabling data-driven decision-making processes, and adopting customer-focused approaches stand out as the fundamental elements of digital transformation strategies. However, in the digital age, leaders' adaptability, leadership styles that encourage innovation, and flexibility are essential for success.

Digital transformation strategies are vital for businesses to gain competitive advantage and ensure sustainable growth. These strategies should not only aim to digitize existing business processes, but also to create new business models and revenue sources. Technologies such as data analytics, artificial intelligence, the IoT and cloud computing, etc. are at the center of this transformation. The transformation of these technologies into usable tools for businesses requires a new leadership approach that can meet the requirements of the age.

Leadership in the digital age requires a more dynamic, innovative and flexible approach than traditional leadership. In today's world, leaders must adapt quickly to technological changes, make data-driven decisions and encourage their teams to learn continuously. These qualities are conceptualized as digital leadership in leadership literature. Digital leaders are individuals who have the knowledge, skills and competencies necessary to manage digital transformation processes and increase organizational success by effectively using digital technologies. In addition, digital leaders focus on goals such as creating innovative business models, increasing efficiency and improving customer experience by using technology as a strategic advantage.

It should not be forgotten that digital transformation is a continuous process. In a world where technology is rapidly evolving, businesses and leaders must constantly follow innovations and update their strategies accordingly. In the future, digital leaders must demonstrate more inclusive and responsible leadership by prioritizing values such as sustainability, diversity and inclusion. In this way, they can make the most of the opportunities brought by the digital age and develop bold ideas for a brave new world.

References

Bharadwaj, A., El Sawy, O. A., Pavlou, P. A., & Venkatraman, N. (2013). Digital business strategy: Toward a next generation of insights. *MIS Quarterly, 37*(2), 471–482.

Blaschke, M., Cigaina, M., Riss, U. V., & Shoshan, I. (2017). Designing business models for the digital economy. *Shaping the Digital Enterprise: Trends and Use Cases in Digital Innovation and Transformation*, 121–136.

Brynjolfsson, E., & McAfee, A. (2014). *The second machine age: Work, progress, and prosperity in a time of brilliant technologies*. W. W. Norton & Company.

Chen, H., Chiang, R. H. L., & Storey, V. C. (2012). Business Intelligence and Analytics: From Big Data to Big Impact. *MIS Quarterly, 36*(4), 1165–1188.

Davenport, T. H., & Ronanki, R. (2018). Artificial intelligence for the real world. *Harvard Business Review, 96*(1), 108–116.

Deloitte. (2015). *Survival Through Digital Leadership*.

Gebayew, C., Hardini, I. R., Panjaitan, G. H. A., & Kurniawan, N. B. (2018, October). A systematic literature review on digital transformation. In *2018 International Conference on Information Technology Systems and Innovation (ICITSI)* (pp. 260–265). IEEE.

Hussain, H. N., Alabdullah, T. T. Y., Ries, E., & Jamal, K. A. M. (2023). Implementing Technology for Competitive Advantage in Digital Marketing. *International Journal of Scientific and Management Research, 6*(6), 95–114.

Zhang, J., Lichtenstein, Y., & Gander, J. (2015). Designing scalable digital business models. In *Business models and modelling* (pp. 241–277). Emerald Group Publishing Limited.

Kurpayanidi, K. (2023). Modern digitalization: priorities and prospects in the context of economic transformation. *Actual Problems of Humanities and Social Sciences, 3*(2), 22–28.

Mihova, T., & Chukalov, K. (2019, October). Digital business models in industrial enterprises. In *IOP Conference Series: Materials Science and Engineering* (Vol. 618, No. 1, p. 012074). IOP Publishing.

Oktaysoy, O., Topcuoğlu, E., & Kaygin, E. (2023). A study on digital leadership scale adaptation. *International Journal of Organizational Leadership*.

Olifirov, A. V., Makoveichuk, K. A., & Petrenko, S. A. (2019). Transformation of business models in the digital economy. *International Journal of Open Information Technologies*, 7(4), 85–91.

Porter, M. E., & Heppelmann, J. E. (2015). How smart, connected products are transforming companies. *Harvard Business Review, 93*(10), 96–114.

Rachinger, M., Rauter, R., Müller, C., Vorraber, W., & Schirgi, E. (2018). Digitalization and its influence on business model innovation. *Journal of manufacturing technology management*, *30*(8), 1143–1160.

Ritter, M., & Schanz, H. (2019). The sharing economy: A comprehensive business model framework. *Journal of cleaner production*, *213*, 320–331.

Seufert, E. B. (2013). *Freemium economics*: Leveraging analytics and user segmentation to drive revenue. Elsevier.

Shehadeh, M., Almohtaseb, A., Aldehayyat, J., & Abu-AlSondos, I. A. (2023). Digital transformation and competitive advantage in the service sector: a moderated-mediation model. *Sustainability*, *15*(3), 2077.

Shpylyk, S., Pinyak, I., & Shveda, N. (2021). Digital marketing as an innovative control element: development by evolution.

Teece, D. J. (2010). Business models, business strategy and innovation. *Long range planning*, 43(2–3), 172–194.

Topcuoğlu, E., Oktaysoy, O., Erdoğan, S. U., Kaygin, E., & Karafakioğlu, E. (2023). The mediating role of job security in the impact of digital leadership on job satisfaction and life satisfaction. *Marketing and Management of Innovations*.

Verhoef, P. C., Broekhuizen, T., Bart, Y., Bhattacharya, A., Dong, J. Q., Fabian, N., & Haenlein, M. (2019). Digital transformation: A multidisciplinary reflection and research agenda. *Journal of Business Research*, 122, 889–901.

Westerman, G., & Bonnet, D. (2015). Revamping your business through digital transformation. *MIT Sloan management review*, *56*(3), 10.

Zhu, P. (2015). *Digital master: Debunk the myths of enterprise digital maturity*. Lulu Press, Inc.

Zolnowski, A., Anke, J., & Gudat, J. (2017). Towards a cost-benefit-analysis of data-driven business models.

5

Digital Leadership in the Effectiveness of Organizational Crisis Management

Digital Complexity, Scrum, and Agile Leadership

Abdullah Çalışkan[1], İrfan Akkoç[2], and Ömer Turunç[3]

1. Introduction

The emergence of digital technologies has transformed the operations of organizations and their crisis management processes. Digital leadership has gained importance as a critical competency for organizations, and the ability of leaders to leverage technology to enhance decision-making, communication, and efficiency has emerged as a crucial skill. One of the primary responsibilities of digital leaders is to integrate digital tools and platforms into crisis management strategies. This integration enables organizations to respond to crises in a more agile and rapid manner. Digital leadership is not just about managing technology, but also about strategically positioning the organization for success in a digital-first world.

This section examines the multifaceted role of digital leaders within organizations, highlighting the skills and qualities required for effective leadership in crisis situations. It also aims to help organizations understand the broader implications of digital leadership and agile methodologies in crisis management, providing guidance for future research and practice.

1 Prof. Dr. Toros University, <abdullah.caliskan@toros.edu.tr>
2 Assoc. Prof., İzmir Tınaztepe University, <dr.irfanakkoc@gmail.com>
3 Prof. Dr. Antalya Science University, <omer.turunc@antalya.edu.tr>

2. Understanding Digital Complexity in Crisis Management

Digital complexity refers to the multifaceted and interconnected nature of digital environments, characterized by technological advancements, and the proliferation of digital devices. This complexity presents both opportunities and challenges for organizations, particularly in the context of crisis management.

One of the primary dimensions of digital complexity is technological interdependence. Organizations rely on interconnected systems and platforms, creating a web of dependencies that can amplify the impact of a crisis (Bass & Avolio, 1994). For example, cybersecurity breach can spread to other areas. This requires organizations to adopt a holistic approach to crisis management.

Another critical dimension is that the volume and variety of data generated by digital systems can overwhelm traditional crisis management processes (Kouzes & Posner, 2017). Organizations must develop the capability to analyze large datasets, using advanced analytics. Digital complexity encompasses the evolving nature of digital threats. Cyber threats are constantly changing, with new vulnerabilities and attack vectors emerging regularly (Chinthapatla, 2024). This requires leveraging threat intelligence.

Understanding digital complexity is essential for crisis management in the digital age. Organizations must recognize the multifaceted nature of digital environments and develop strategies to manage evolving threats. Digital complexity presents challenges. One of them is the speed at which digital crises can escalate. Due to the nature of digital systems, a small issue can quickly become a significant crisis, requiring rapid response and decision-making (Kreps, 2020). This requires collaboration tools, as well as effective coordination.

The interconnected nature of digital systems means that a crisis in one area can have far-reaching effects across the organization (Park & Mithas, 2020). Organizations must have the capability to conduct comprehensive impact assessments. In conclusion, digital complexity poses challenges for organizations. To address these, organizations must develop the capability to detect and respond to digital threats. The utilization of digital tools is essential. Advanced monitoring tools provide real-time visibility, enabling organizations to detect potential vulnerabilities before they escalate into crises (Avolio, Sosik, Kahai, & Baker, 2014). Effective communication and collaboration tools are also critical. These tools enable crisis management teams to collaborate effectively.

Digital analytics and reporting tools can help organizations conduct these reviews more efficiently. Organizations can use these insights to refine their crisis management strategies and improve their resilience to future crises (Blackburn, LaBerge, O'Toole, & Schneider, 2020). In conclusion, the strategic utilization of digital tools is essential for effective crisis detection and response. This section highlights the importance of digital tools in crisis management, providing a foundation for the subsequent discussions on agile methodologies and digital leadership.

3. Applying Scrum and Agile Leadership During Crisis

Although Scrum and agile practices are used effectively in the software industry, their flexibility and managerial effectiveness are also used in many other industries (Rigby et al., 2016). Scrum's efficiencies in transparency, review and adaptation are crucial for managing chaos in crises caused by uncertainty and rapid change.

Agile methodologies have a scope that includes adaptability, collaboration and customer-oriented practices (Betra et al., 2017). In addition, agile methodologies recommend the creation of cross-functional teams that bring together interdisciplinary skills and views (Khalil et al., 2013). In crisis management, these cross-functional teams are an important factor in strengthening the management process to deal with highly chaotic situations by gathering expert knowledge from different disciplines. Using agile practices for stressful environments in crisis management also requires anticipating different situations due to the nature of the crisis. In a crisis environment, these practices enable faster reaction and adaptation to new situations through rapidly changing conditions and shorter sprints teams. In other words, agile practices support more informed and rapid decision-making in sensitive, high-stress environments (Pfeiffer et al., 2019).

In summary, agile applications support decision-making processes in high-stress environments and support adaptation by helping the solution. It supports this through shorter sprints with fast communication and decision-making, setting the right priorities and developing a culture of resilience.

These adaptations enable teams to remain agile and responsive in the dynamic, high-pressure environment of the crisis.

4. The Critical Role of Digital Leaders in Managing Crises

Digital leaders play a crucial role in managing crises. These leaders have an understanding of digital tools and platforms, enabling them to integrate technology into crisis management (Schwaber & Sutherland, 2017). Another important trait is strategic thinking. Leaders must be able to anticipate potential crises and develop strategies to mitigate risks (Hassan & Hamed, 2022a). This involves recognizing threats and developing comprehensive crisis management.

Effective communication skills are also essential. During a crisis, clear communication is critical (Bass & Avolio, 1994). Digital leaders must be able to articulate the organization's crisis response strategy. Crises are unpredictable, and leaders must be able to adapt to changing circumstances (Kouzes & Posner, 2017). This requires a mindset of continuous learning, as well as the ability to remain calm under pressure.

Digital leaders leverage technology to enhance communication (Kim, 2021). For example, digital collaboration tools can facilitate information sharing among crisis management teams, enabling more effective responses. Similarly, data analytics platforms can provide actionable insights that support informed decision-making and strategic planning. Contingency plans are another way to improve robustness. These plans outline the responsibilities of crisis management teams, establish protocols for responding to different types of crises, and identify critical resources and support systems (Brown, 2020). By having these frameworks in place, organizations are better prepared for crises. To illustrate the critical role of digital leaders in managing crises, several leaders who have excelled in this area have been used as examples. The first one is Satya Nadella, CEO of Microsoft. Under his leadership, Microsoft has successfully navigated several crises, including cybersecurity threats and market disruptions. His focus on fostering a culture of continuous learning and innovation has been instrumental in driving the company's success during crises.

Another example is Mary Barra, CEO of General Motors. Barra has led the company through significant crises (Schein, 2010). Her effective communication skills and ability to make quick, informed decisions have been key to the company's crisis management efforts. The characteristics, skills, and strategies of digital leaders provide valuable insight into how they can manage complex and dynamic situations and achieve successful outcomes for their organizations (Klus & Müller, 2021).

5. Strategic Decision Making in Crisis Situations

The decision-making process during crises needs both speed and precision. Digital tools increase the speed and accuracy of the decision-making process through the availability of real-time data, advanced analytics, and decision-support capabilities (Brynjolfsson and McAfee, 2014). Among the chief assets of digital tools is the capacity to deliver insights on the spot or in real time to significant data and tendencies. The second critical capacity of digital tools is scenario planning and simulation support. The decision support tools will model different scenarios and estimate their possible outcome, thus helping the teams to weigh the best course of action (Snowden and Boone, 2007) Digital communication tools also enhance decision-making. This is done through the provision of real-time collaboration and sharing of information. In any crisis, all relevant stakeholders need access to accurate and timely information (Schwaber and Sutherland, 2017).

Agile decision-making frameworks are important in managing crises because they provide structured yet flexible approaches to decision-making. They help a crisis management team respond effectively to dynamic and unpredictable situations by accounting for cycles, continuous feedback, and rapid adjustments. One of the key precepts of agile decision-making is that it is handled in iterative cycles or sprints. For crisis management, this offers teams an opportunity for appraisal of status, execution of measures for responses, and checking the effectiveness of these measures at very short intervals. Other key factors of agile decision-making include feedback and data. The crisis management team should, from time to time, review their actions and outcomes, and seek feedback from members of the team and other stakeholders (Waller et al., 2013; Kouzes and Posner, 2017). The rapid adjustment is another key ingredient for agile decision-making in crisis management. Crises are intrinsically uncertain, and teams need to respond flexibly to new information and shifting circumstances (Goleman, 1998; Richtnér et al. 2017).

One very important element of effective crisis management is post-crisis analysis. According to Van der Voet, it deals with reviewing the actions taken during the crisis, assessing their consequences, and drawing lessons that can be referred to in attempts at managing future crises (Van der Voet, 2014). One major constituent element for post-crisis analysis is decision-making process evaluation. Organizations should scrutinize crisis-time decisions in the light of available information and the consequences of those decisions. The second important part refers to an evaluation of the response effort. Organizations have to assess various actions taken to handle a crisis, including how effective the communication, coordination, and resource allocation activities were during the response effort. This is a crucial approach for organizations to identify best practice and improve their crisis management strategies to increase resilience. Stakeholder assessments are also crucial for post-crisis process evaluation and feedback. This is because feedback from employees, consumers and other stakeholders is important in determining managerial effectiveness in crisis management.

Feedback is therefore useful in determining how the crisis is perceived and the effectiveness of management in managing this process. Stakeholder feedback is an important tool to identify their expectations and needs and to support their inclusion in the crisis management process and to improve crisis management effectiveness.

6. Conclusion

In the ever-evolving digital landscape, organizations face increasing complexity in managing crises, making digital leadership a pivotal factor in ensuring successful outcomes. The role of digital leaders extends beyond mere technological management; they must foster agility, strategic foresight, and resilience to navigate crises effectively. By understanding and managing digital complexity, organizations can mitigate risks and respond swiftly to emerging threats. Agile methodologies, such as Scrum, offer a flexible framework that enables crisis management teams to adapt quickly, ensuring efficient decision-making under pressure. The iterative nature of agile leadership, with its emphasis on collaboration, rapid response, and constant feedback, proves invaluable during unpredictable crises.

Digital tools further enhance crisis management by providing real-time data, supporting decision-making processes, and enabling cross-functional collaboration. These technologies allow organizations to anticipate crises, simulate potential scenarios, and optimize their responses. Successful crisis management in today's digital age hinges on the ability of leaders to navigate the complex digital environment while fostering a culture of continuous learning, collaboration, and agility. Organizations that invest in digital leadership, agile frameworks, and advanced technologies are better equipped to handle crises, ensuring long-term sustainability and resilience in the face of future challenges.

References

Avolio, B. J., Sosik, J. J., Kahai, S. S., & Baker, B. (2014). E-Leadership: Re-Examining Transformations in Leadership Source and Transmission. The Leadership Quarterly, 25(1), 105–131.

Bass, B. M., & Avolio, B. J. (1994). Improving Organizational Effectiveness through Transformational Leadership. SAGE Publications.

Blackburn, S., LaBerge, L., O'Toole, C., & Schneider, J. (2020). Digital strategy in a time of crisis. McKinsey Digital, April 22.

Brown, B. (2020). Dare to Lead: Brave Work. Tough Conversations. Whole Hearts. Random House.

Brynjolfsson, E., & McAfee, A. (2014). The Second Machine Age: Work, Progress, and Prosperity in a Time of Brilliant Technologies. W. W. Norton & Company.

Chinthapatla, Y. (2024). Mastering Digital Complexity: The Role of Configuration Management Database (CMDB) in Modern Infrastructure Management. Journal Homepage: <http://www. ijmra. us, 14(03)>

Gartner. (2019). Gartner Identifies the Top 10 Strategic Technology Trends for 2020. Retrieved from <https://www.gartner.com/en/newsroom/press-releases/2019-10-21-gartner-identifies-the-top-10-strategic-technology-trends-for-2020>

Gill, R. (2002). Change Management--or Change Leadership? Journal of Change Management, 3(4), 307–318. DOI:10.1080/714023845

Goleman, D. (1998). What Makes a Leader? Harvard Business Review.

Hassan, N. K., & Hamed, S. A. (2022). The impact of digital leadership in the effectiveness of organizational crisis management by mediating strategic vigilance. Journal of Economics and Administrative Sciences, 28(133), 1–20.

Hassan, N. K., & Hamed, S. A. (2022). The role of digital leadership in the effectiveness of organizational crisis management. Journal of Positive School Psychology, 5373–5379.

Hayward, S. (2021). The agile leader: how to create an agile business in the digital age (2nd ed.). Harlow, England: Pearson Education Limited

Kim, C. M. (2021). Leveraging Technology in Leadership Communication (1st ed.). Routledge. DOI:10.4324/9781003224655

Klus, M. F., & Müller, J. (2021). The digital leader: what one needs to master today's organisational challenges. Journal of Business Economics, 91(8), 1189–1223.

Kouzes, J. M., & Posner, B. Z. (2017). The Leadership Challenge (7th ed.). Jossey-Bass.

Kreps, G. (2020). The COVID-19 Infodemic and Digital Health Literacy. Journal of Consumer Health on the Internet, 24(2), 120–128.

Ly, B. (2023). The interplay of digital transformational leadership, organizational agility, and digital transformation. Journal of the Knowledge Economy, 1–20.

Park, Y., & Mithas, S. (2020). Organized complexity of digital business strategy: A configurational perspective. Mis Quarterly, 44(1).

Pfeiffer, & Sauer, & Ritter, (2019). Agile methods as stress management tools? An empirical study. Work Organisation, Labour & Globalisation. 13. 20. 10.13169/workorgalaboglob.13.2.0020.

Schein, E. H. (2010). Organizational Culture and Leadership. CA, USA, John Wiley & Sons.

Schwaber, K., & Sutherland, J. (2017). The Scrum Guide: The Definitive Guide to Scrum: The Rules of the Game. Scrum.org.

Snowden, D. J., & Boone, M. E. (2007). A Leader's Framework for Decision Making. Harvard Business Review.

Van der Voet, J. (2014). The Effectiveness and Specificity of Change Management in a Public Organization: Transformational Leadership and a Bureaucratic Organizational Structure. European Management Journal, 32(3), 373–382.

Waller, Mary & Lei, Zhike & Pratten, Robert. (2013). Focusing on Teams in Crisis Management Education: An Integration and Simulation-Based Approach. Academy of Management Learning & Education. 13. 208–221. 10.5465/amle.2012.0337.

6

Digital Leadership Within the Scope of Corporate Leadership Introduction

Pınar Fayganoğlu[1] & Rukiye Yalçın[2]

1. The Concept of Digital Leadership

Industry has been defined as a highly important force that influences the socio-economic structure of every era and society that has experienced it from the past to the present. The evolution of such an important force has been shaped by industrial revolutions characterized by a series of stages and innovations. The rapid developments in information and communication technologies integrated into production processes have led to the reshaping of traditional industrial structures. This situation has initiated an evolutionary process in organizational terms. Industry 4.0, referred to as the new phase of digitalization and the transformation of industry, signifies the integration of smart devices that can communicate independently within the value chain (Santos et al., 2018). The evolution of digital technologies reflects a long process that has taken years. While it can be said that many technologies still do not have a wide range of applications today, the existence of available and secure technologies for some industrial applications is an undeniable reality.

Industry 4.0 aims to integrate corporate machinery, production equipment, and cyber-physical systems. It is stated that this integration process enables organizations to automatically exchange information and automatically control their actions and controls (Hou et al, 2020). Therefore, it can be said that this approach will bring radical improvements in production

1 Assoc. Prof., The National Defense University Army War School <pfayganoglu@kho.msu.edu.tr>
2 Assoc. Prof., The National Defense University Army War School <rcyalcin@kho.msu.edu.tr>

processes, engineering applications, material management, supply chain optimization, and industrial operations as a whole. Especially in the digital transformation, which can be said to have started with Industry 4.0, there is a need for a team with hardware and capabilities that can keep up with this process, as technical information is being integrated into research and development, and supply chain applications. In this context, the concept of digital transformation should be seen not only as trying technological developments and innovations, but as an effort to move all systems and activities to the digital environment on a broader scale (Coelho et al., 2023). In other words, digital transformation is defined as a period in which both business and information technology innovations are more integrated, and a more digital perspective is adopted from a corporate information technology perspective (Klein, 2020). Furthermore, in this process, the necessity of integrating digital technologies such as social media, artificial intelligence, and big data applications into all kinds of business processes within the enterprise and developing new business models within this framework stands out. In order for businesses to manage their digital transformation processes, they need to adopt central digital transformation strategies that affect information technologies, business development processes, and every unit/department operating within the structure. This situation introduces us to the concept of digital business management, referring to the transformation that businesses undergo using information technologies. This concept, defined as a digital enterprise, has developed in the new economic environment that places information at the center and advocates that innovation is the sole fundamental dynamic of change, unlike the classical business structure. It represents a comprehensive process of change that extends from the main job description of the business to how the work is done and the networks of relationships established with stakeholders (Soule et al., 2016; Kontić & Vidicki, 2018; Chatterjee et al., 2023). In this context, it can be said that these structures defined as digital enterprises have been able to integrate their activities and processes with information technologies, including the impact of technology on business activities and processes. However, as much as the business process understands and is willing to integrate its activities, it is stated that the biggest challenge encountered in the implementation of digital transformation at the business level is the employees (Chatterjee et al., 2023). Failing to engage employees or to align all employees in the same direction leads to the failure of digital transformation initiatives. In this context, it is clear that leaders are responsible for managing and monitoring the innovations, applications, and processes that digital transformation will bring about in organizations, and for guiding employees in the same direction within the defined goals and objectives that can lead businesses to success. At this point, it is emphasized that leadership capabilities and the operational implementation of digital transformation, referred to as the two important aspects (Westerman et al., 2014). Being able to have a transformative digital vision, providing motivation through employee participation, focusing on digital governance, and creating technological leadership abilities are listed as leadership skills necessary for digital success. Some of these characteristics are also considered accepted characteristics for other leadership approaches. In addition to the qualities possessed by the leader, the operational implementation of leadership is another important aspect to consider. Within the digital transformation process, operational leadership practices involve several stages. These can be listed as identifying digital challenges, focusing on investment, and mobilizing the organization. In the first stage of identifying digital challenges, the leader starts by creating a team with the necessary vision that is suitable for the digital transformation process the organization is in, to raise awareness among this team about the digital opportunities and threats they may encounter. The second stage, focusing on investment, involves the leader preparing an implementation method that includes the necessary funding for all elements to function flawlessly after creating the vision. The third and final stage, mobilizing the organization, includes creating a sense of urgency within the organization by highlighting the goal, purpose, and necessary elements through open communication channels, encouraging workforce participation to achieve rapid impact, and creating new behavioral patterns.

2. Digital Leadership As a New Management Style in Organizations

It is clear that the first requirement for organizations to adapt to digital transformation is change management, and leaders play a crucial role in successfully managing this change. However, due to the nature of the transformation process, the changes it creates in business strategy and talent perceptions have led to the need for leaders with different structures and characteristics from traditional leadership styles. This new style of leadership, defined as digital leadership, refers to the ability to develop and implement strategies within digital transformation processes (DeAraujo et al., 2021) and can be described as an essential element of institutionalization in the digital age (Gartner et al., 2024). Adapting to this digital transformation and integrating all the mechanisms of the organization into it can only be achieved through successful change management practices. Traditional hierarchical leadership styles have proven to be inadequate in leading digital transformation processes that require relatively more flexibility in business strategies, leading to the necessity for a new style of leadership with different capabilities and skills. In response to this need, it can be said that in recent years, in addition to traditional command-and-control and visionary leadership styles, a third-generation leadership approach called digital leadership has emerged. While most traditional leadership models are built on a certain authority, hierarchy, and focus on control, digital leadership adopts a more collaborative, flexible, proactive, and easily adaptable approach (Prince, 2017). However, within the concept of digital transformation, it is necessary to consider not only the changes in technology or related changes in business processes but also the changes in organizational cultures, employee skills, and leadership styles. Industry 4.0 refers to a transformation process that fundamentally changes organizations, their production processes, and business models. In this increasingly competitive environment, the survival of businesses will only be possible through successful management practices (Prince, 2018). It is expected that digital leadership, which is assumed to contribute to the development of a leadership understanding suitable for the requirements and characteristics of the information age, will have different definitions developed by various researchers in the management and organizational research literature.

El Sawy and colleagues (2016) define digital leadership as individuals who can develop the right strategies for businesses to adapt to the digital age and thereby lead the organization to success. Scheninger (2019) defines digital leadership as individuals who can use technology correctly in the context of the organization's goals. The leadership approach defined within the concept implies the ability to see technology not only as a tool but also as a fundamental building block of the business (Benitez et al., 2022). Moreover, digital leadership does not only relate to the technological knowledge that the leader possesses or is expected to have; it also refers to continuously improving leadership skills, using technological knowledge in strategic decision-making, and having effective communication skills while enhancing the overall performance of the business (Porfírio et al., 2021). It is also important for future digital leaders to be able to vertically integrate diverse working teams/teams with different functions and develop innovative collaboration methods. As digital leadership trends affect organizations in a micro context due to the increasing digitalization on a societal scale, tracking every technological development within the organization, adapting to generational differences, and rapidly changing business dynamics require a flexible, fast, and effective leadership approach. Petry (2018) describes digital leadership as an approach related to integrating any technological advancements brought by our era into corporate performance and success. This relatively new approach is concerned with turning information technologies into a strategic advantage and the innovative ability necessary for inter-organizational sustainable competition. Therefore, it can be said that digital leadership is not only about the effective use of technological tools but also about how these tools can be strategically integrated to help organizations achieve their goals. Similarly, Sackett (cited in Baker, 2014), who suggests that digital leadership is not only about technological competencies but also about strategic thinking abilities, argues that digital leaders need to stand out not only with their ability to understand technology but also with their ability to implement big ideas. This highlights the visionary and innovative aspects of digital leaders alongside their practical skills.

In digital leadership, concepts such as trust, collaboration through learning, self-discipline, and communication are extremely important, but characteristics such as innovation, continuous learning, future orientation, and going beyond standard practices can also be considered among the key traits of digital leaders. Digital leaders are highly successful in dealing with challenges (Tigre et al., 2023). They see digitalization not as a result of a situation, but as a tool. Most importantly, they also transform their followers toward this mindset. Additionally, they are highly successful in aspects such as delegation of authority and empowering subordinates. This leadership style primarily focuses on leveraging communication and information technologies to the highest level to increase the effectiveness and efficiency of businesses. However, unlike other leadership styles, it enables this situation either by establishing virtual teams or by allowing employees to work in any environment without the constraints of location and time pressure.

This is why digital leaders tend to move away from centralization and are inclined to create high-performing work teams/groups through collaboration (Jakubik and Beazhny, 2017). Individually, digital leaders are highly interested not only in the information itself but also in the source of the information. Westerman and colleagues (2014) emphasize in their study that digital leaders need to possess certain characteristics. These include the ability to improve decision-making processes, assist their subordinates in this regard, advocate for a culture of collaboration, adapt to change, continuously motivate and guide their subordinates, and effectively deal with uncertainties, thus being problem solvers. Similarly, Promsri (2019) also underscores that digital leaders need to have certain qualities within the organization they are part of for a successful digital transformation process. These qualities are defined as digital literacy, vision, customer orientation, agility, risk-taking, and collaboration. The first quality, digital literacy, signifies the leader's understanding of digital transformation and the supporting technologies, as well as their knowledge level in this regard.

Following information, leaders should have a clear vision and mission related to digital transformation. While doing all this, they should also pay attention to customers' needs and demands, understanding that digital transformation not only affects the organization but also brings changes for the customers. In the rapidly changing global competitive environment, one of the most important qualities that digital leaders need to have to adapt to the environment is agility. Risk-taking, defined as the fifth quality, refers to the digital leader's willingness to seek out new opportunities and not hesitate to capitalize on them when the right opportunity arises. Collaboration, the final quality, requires digital leaders to create a collaborative structure with employees throughout the entire digital transformation process for the success of the organization.

The key condition for the success of digital leaders is defined as change (Shibru & Darshan, 2012), and dynamism, which can be defined as the ability to quickly adapt the organization to changing environmental conditions, is an extremely important aspect. However, the effective implementation of dynamism and the organization's full realization of it depend on making the organizational culture dynamic as well (Attafar et al., 2013). In this leadership approach, leaders have the ability to see and analyze the opportunities and challenges presented by the digital transformation process. The sustainable competitive advantage provided to businesses by technology and digitalization necessitates organizations to set a digitalization goal, and it is the responsibility of digital leaders to guide the organization on how to reach this goal. As a result of the many challenges encountered in directing transformation, developing strategies, and implementing them, it has become necessary to identify the characteristics and behavioral patterns that leaders need to facilitate the organization's transition to digitalization.

Leaders of the digital age are expected to be equipped with the necessary knowledge and skills to meet social expectations. However, it is not enough to reveal only the characteristic features of these new style leaders; their technical knowledge, skills and technological literacy are also extremely crucial. In today's rapidly changing societies where competition has evolved to different levels, it is vital for businesses to integrate all their functions into digital processes in order to survive.

3. Digital Leadership Within the Scope of Corporate Leadership

The first studies related to the traditional corporate leadership model can be said to have started with the works of Weber (1978) and Durkheim, which put forward what institutions are and how they affect/shape action and structure within the context of social patterns such as beliefs and norms. Weber (1978), considered one of the founders of the institutional school, assigns a subjective meaning to the actor through cultural systems and emphasizes the sociality of action within this framework. Although the concept of corporate leadership existed, especially in the comparison of corporate and personal leadership styles, as seen in Neumann's work (1941) during that period, it was in later periods that studies were conducted on how organizations became institutions and how institutional processes affected organizations. Selznick (1996), considered the founder of institutional theory, identified various leadership functions that should be present in the process of transforming an organization into an institution. Subsequently, with his work "Leadership in Administration" (1957), Selznick fully introduced the concept of corporate leadership into the literature. Selznick describes the corporate leader as a statesman and assigns some important tasks to top executives within this framework. These tasks are defined as being able to create value, develop it, spread these values, make them sustainable, protect them, and materialize them. In distinguishing between organization and institution, Selznick (1984) suggests that the most important point in an organization becoming an institution is taking social needs into account and making the organization adaptable. In this context, being able to be a corporate leader not only involves embodying the values and goals of the organization in the social structure but also being able to see that these are internalized in the behavior of others.

Selznick (1957; 1984) portrays the corporate leader as someone who can make critical decisions, being both the most important factor in institutionalization and the organization's fundamental protector as a social entity. In addition, two types of corporate leadership definitions can be observed. The first one is responsible leadership, which can be defined as a blend of loyalty, understanding, and determination. The statesmanship attributed to the corporate leader stems directly from this sense of corporate responsibility. Within this sense of responsibility, a different definition of leadership is made by adding roles of change and restructuring. This second model, defined as creative corporate leadership, describes the process where individual and all kinds of technological inputs are processed to embody new and lasting values of the organization, thereby reconstructing the institution in this way. This type of leadership primarily emphasizes a more dynamic process that continuously renews the organization. In fact, it is also reported that this dynamism over time transforms a manager into a statesman transitioning from mere administrative activities to corporate leadership (Selznick, 1957).

When examining modern studies on corporate leadership, it is observed that different meanings are attributed to the corporate leader. For example, while Podolny and colleagues (2004) assign a new role to the corporate leader in terms of instilling purpose and meaning, Kraatz (2009) suggests that a new vision and mission to be created within the organization can only be achieved by corporate leaders and they mention five different types of corporate leadership. These are visionary leadership, persuasive leadership, sustainable leadership, flexible leadership, coalition network leadership, and persuasive leadership.

4. Conclusion

The digital developments, the increasingly uncertain nature of the environment, and the evolution of societies have necessitated some changes in organizational and management structures simultaneously. Many different methods used by leaders to show that any role attributed to corporate leadership and leaders are much more than a "established political structure of an organization" are almost losing their validity for today. One of the main reasons for this is the transition to a new social era called the digital transformation age. In a period of rapidly changing, technology-driven uncertainties, it is evaluated that the success of organizations will only be possible if corporate leaders focus on how to integrate their organizations into these new developments. With the spread of digital transformation through Industry 4.0 and even Industry 5.0, it can be said that businesses need leaders who can combine many different leadership qualities in a single structure, rather than a single type of leader with traditional logic. In this context, it can be said that the survival and success of businesses in the newly emerging social order depend on digital leaders integrated into corporate leadership, which plays a crucial role in turning organizations into institutions.

References

Attafar, A., Sadidi, M., Attafar, H., & Shahin, A. (2013). The role of customer knowledge management (CKM) in improving organization-customer relationships. Middle-East Journal of Scientific Research, 13(6), 829–835. DOI:10.5829/idosi. mejsr.2013.13.6.2533

Baker, M. (2014). Digital transformation. Createspace Independent P.

Benitez, J., Arenas, A., Castillo, A., & Esteves, J. (2022). Impact of digital leadership capability on innovation performance: The role of platform digitization capability. Information & Management, 59(2), 103590.

Chatterjee, S., Chaudhuri, R., Vrontis, D., & Giovando, G. (2023). Digital workplace and organization performance: Moderating role of digital leadership capability. Journal of Innovation & Knowledge, 8(1), 100334.

Coelho, P., Bessa, C., Landeck, J., & Silva, C. (2023). Industry 5.0: the arising of a concept. Procedia Computer Science, 217, 1137–1144.

DeAraujo, L. M., Priadana, S., Paramarta, V., & Sunarsi, D. (2021). Digital leadership in business organizations. International Journal of Educational Administration, Management, and Leadership, 45–56.

El Sawy, O. A., Kraemmergaard, P., Amsinck, H., and Vinther, A. L. (2016). How LEGO Built the Foundations and Enterprise Capabilities for Digital Leadership. MIS Quarterly Executive, 15(2),141–166.

Gartner, J., Maresch, D., & Tierney, R. (2024). The key to scaling in the digital era: Simultaneous automation, individualization and interdisciplinarity. Journal of Small Business Management, 62(2), 628–655.

Hou, T., Cheng, B., Wang, R., Xue, W., & Chaudhry, P. E. (2020). Developing Industry 4.0 with systems perspectives. Systems Research and Behavioral Science, 37(4), 741–748.

Jakubik, M., & Berazhny, I. (2017). Rethinking leadership and it´ s practices in the digital Era. In Managing the Global Economy. Proceedings of the Management International Conference, Monastier di Treviso, Italy, 24–27 May, 2017.. University of Primorska Press.

Klein, M. (2020). Leadership characteristics in the era of digital transformation.

Kontić, L., & Vidicki, Đ. (2018). Strategy for digital organization: Testing a measurement tool for digital transformation. Strategic Management, 23(1), 29–35.

Kraatz, M. S. (2009). Leadership as institutional work: A bridge to the other side. Institutional work: Actors and agency in institutional studies of organizations, 59–91.

Neumann, S. (1941). Leadership: institutional and personal. The Journal of Politics, 3(2), 133–153.

Petry, T. (2018). Digital leadership. Knowledge management in digital change: New findings and practical cases, 209–218.

Podolny, J. M., Khurana, R., & Hill-Popper, M. (2004). Revisiting the meaning of leadership. Research in organizational behavior, 26, 1–36.

Porfírio, J. A., Carrilho, T., Felício, J. A., & Jardim, J. (2021). Leadership characteristics and digital transformation. Journal of Business Research, 124, 610–619.

Prince, K. A. (2017). Industrie 4.0 and leadership.

Prince, K. A. (2018). Digital leadership: transitioning into the digital age (Doctoral dissertation, James Cook University).

Promsri, C. (2019). The developing model of digital leadership for a successful digital transformation. GPH-International Journal of Business Management, 2(08), 01–08.

Santos, B. P., Charrua-Santos, F., & Lima, T. M. (2018, July). Industry 4.0: an overview. In Proceedings of the World Congress on engineering (Vol. 2, pp. 4–6). IAEN, London, UK.

Selznick, P. 1957. Leadership in administration: A sociological interpretation. New York: Harper & Row

Selznick, P. 1984. Leadership in administration. Berkeley, CA: University of California Press.

Selznick P. (1996). Institutionalism "Old" and "New," Administrative Science Quarterly, Vol: 41(2), pp. 270–277

Selznick, P. (2011). Leadership in administration: A sociological interpretation. Quid Pro Books.

Sheninger, E. (2019). Digital leadership: Changing paradigms for changing times. Corwin Press.

Shibru, B. & Darshan, G. M. (2011). Transformational and its relationship with subordinate satisfaction with leader (The case of Leather Industry in Ethiopia). Interdisciplinary Journal of Contemporary Research in Business, 3(5), 686–697

Soule, D. L., Puram, A., Westerman, G. F., & Bonnet, D. (2016). Becoming a digital organization: The journey to digital dexterity. Available at SSRN 2697688.

Tigre, F. B., Curado, C., & Henriques, P. L. (2023). Digital leadership: A bibliometric analysis. Journal of leadership & organizational studies, 30(1), 40–70.

Westerman, G., Bonnet, D., & McAfee, A. (2014). Leading digital: Turning technology into business transformation. Harvard Business Press.
Weber, M. (1978), The Theory of Social and Economic Organization, Free Press, New York, NY, (T. Parsons, Trans.).

7

Digital Leaders in Digital Learning Organizations

How Is the Learning Environment Changing?

Tuğrul Oğuzhan[1]

1. Introduction to Digital Leaders in Digital Learning Organizations

Progress in technology is having a big impact on the competitiveness of businesses. This includes new ways of doing business, new competition, new products, and more automation in processes because of new technology. It is also essential for companies to move away from traditional learning and development in favor of fully embracing the digital age and becoming digital learning organizations. The process starts within the organization, driven by digital leaders who are leading innovation and spearheading the digital revolution. Their main goal is to create a skilled and knowledgeable digital workforce that can thrive in today's rapidly changing digital world (Zaoui and Souissi, 2020).

In the digital age, leadership is key to guiding organizations and companies must have efficient technical systems for production, communication, and cost savings to remain competitive. Digital leaders drive digital transformation initiatives, promoting agility, efficiency, and customer-centricity in an ever-evolving digital landscape. By embracing change and supporting digital strategies, they inspire teams to adapt, innovate, and continuously evolve (Sağbaş and Erdoğan, 2022; Veithzal and Rony, 2024).

Online courses, training platforms, webinars, interactive modules and virtual simulations are widely used as digital learning tools. These resources provide employees with training and development opportunities, allowing

1 Assoc. Prof., OSTIM Technical University, <tugrul.oguzhan@ostimteknik.edu.tr>

them to acquire new skills and knowledge. In addition, digital learning activities encourage collaboration and knowledge sharing among employees, creating a culture of continuous learning within the organization (Chatterjee et al., 2023).

The relationship between digital leaders and the digital learning environment is of great importance. Today, effective digital leaders demonstrate five key qualities: adaptability, rapid response to challenges, foresight, empowerment and motivation of others, and resilience. These qualities underlie their success in navigating the ever-changing digital environment with confidence. The digital learning environment supported by the digital leader therefore ensures the successful integration of technology and enhances the educational experience for everyone involved (McCarthy et al.,2022; Erhan et al., 2022; Benitez et al., 2022).

2. The Evolving Learning Environment and the Role of Digital Leaders

Senge is known for originating the idea of the learning organization, with five key principles for constructing and nurturing learning organizations: 1. Continuous Learning. 2. Shared Vision. 3. Open Communication. 4. Experimentation and Innovation. 5. Empowered and Engaged Employees. By applying these principles, organizations can handle complexity, constantly improve, and guarantee long-term sustainability (Hsu and Lamb, 2020; Reese, 2020). In 2017, Overton and some other scholars outlined six more essential elements: Clear Purpose, Holistic individual growth, Thriving environment, Agile tech-enabled structure, Continuous engagement, and Intelligent decision-making. Their contributions have transformed organizational learning into digital learning (Alerasoul et al., 2022; Ivaldi et al., 2022).

In the era of Industry 4.0 and digitalization, there is often a strong emphasis on technological advancements, and in the field of digital learning, much attention has been given to the use of technology to support knowledge sharing, collaboration, and access to learning materials (Meier et al., 2021). In this era, digital leaders possess the expertise and vision to harness the power of technology such as artificial intelligence, virtual reality, and big data analytics to enhance teaching methodologies, empower educators, engage students, and create personalized and immersive learning experiences

(McCarthy et al., 2023; Ruël et al., 2021). It is important to recognize that a lack of integration of Industry 4.0 technologies can disrupt organizational routines and hinder further digital operations and automation initiatives. At that point, digital leadership style involves the introduction and operation of software (software, applications, operating systems) and hardware (cell phones, modems, computers, touch screens), work ethic, and legal issues in information technology (Tortorella et al., 2020; Ruël et al., 2021). A digital leader also has an important place in their contributions to the transfer of developments of the information sector to society. Therefore, to seize these advantages and turn them into opportunities, embracing digital leadership is very important in order to direct the appropriate use of new technologies and promote equality and effectiveness in education (Musaigwa and Kalitanyi, 2024; Ahlquist, 2020).

3. Impact of Digital Leaders on Learning Organizations

It is essential for digital leaders to stay up to date on the latest developments and changes in the digital business environment and to use digital resources in personal and professional environments. In addition, these leaders need to prioritize ongoing digital education for themselves and their team members, focusing on key areas such as big data and analytics, cloud computing, IoT, AI, e-commerce, online and social media marketing, and smart mobile technologies to achieve sustainable growth, to remain competitive, and to stay abreast of developments in today's digitally driven world (McCarthy et al., 2023; Yansen and Yujie, 2023).

Leadership 4.0, also known as digital leadership, is an accelerated, collaborative, and team-oriented strategy that prioritizes innovation. The leader's personal skills, mindset, and openness to implementing new methods such as design thinking are essential for Leadership 4.0. By adopting this style, leaders can unleash the full potential of their teams and achieve meaningful results (Anak and Sri, 2020; Haleem et al., 2024). Digital leadership involves leading in key areas of the information society, such as communication, journalism, and various media. It is important for digital leaders to not only recognize the potential of technology for leading a company but also understand the limitations of these tools and how they impact leadership at all levels of the organization (Klein, 2020).

Digital leadership aligns with transformational and transactional leadership styles with an emphasis on emotional intelligence. According to Zhang and Zhao (2016), digital leadership facilitates transformational leadership by enhancing communication and engagement through digital platforms. By blending digital and transformational leadership approaches, educational leaders can innovate and lead change using a comprehensive technological approach (Phakamach et al., 2023). Emotional intelligence is crucial for digital leaders to navigate the complexities of remote work and digital interactions. Kane et al. (2015) note that leaders must leverage emotional intelligence to foster collaboration and adaptability within digital environments.

3.1. Enhancing Learning Outcomes Through Digital Initiatives

The training environment may include both formal and informal learning opportunities, and access to resources is controlled and provided by the organization. When it is mentioned about digital learning, it can go by different names such as digital acquisition learning, web-based acquisition training, computer-based training, distance learning, or digital learning. The term digital learning is used for simplicity. In today's business world, digital learning involves utilizing technology to deliver and support web-based instruction, an integrated approach that combines digital learning capabilities, and virtual learning resources to enrich the learning experience (Sousa and Rocha, 2019; Konstantinou, Nachbagauer, and Wehnes, 2023).

The changing external environment of organizations, characterized by global collaboration, virtual business models, and diverse workforces, necessitates changes within organizations as well. In traditional settings, expertise, knowledge, and leadership development are centralized and integrated within formal hierarchies. However, with the shift to digital learning, organizations and leaders have access to a wider range of knowledge and learning opportunities. Digital learning organizations stand out due to their distinct features and technologies. Leaders in these organizations have a unique way of connecting with their teams, creating a web-like network to foster interaction and innovation. The use of social media and collaborative platforms has transformed communication and engagement within these organizations. Businesses that prioritize digital education are often seen as pioneers in their field, renowned for their eagerness to embrace new ideas and their willingness to take risks with innovative concepts (Tortorella et al., 2020; Meier et al., 2021).

Incorporating digital capabilities is essential for improving learning objectives. These objectives may involve providing better learning experiences, combining formal and personalized learning, supporting informal learning, delivering timely learning content, and transitioning to a lifelong learning approach. Therefore, understanding employees' diverse learning needs is vital for achieving learning success, and a one-size-fits-all digitally integrated solution may not be suitable for everyone.

4. Future Trends in Digital Learning

After advances in artificial intelligence, especially in machine learning, smart machines have become more integrated into different work environments; it has been crucial for organizations to effectively utilize and interact with them. This process of organizational digital learning occurs at the individual level (developing fusion skills), the technological level (using various forms of machine learning to enhance algorithms), and the organizational level (creating a culture of rethinking business processes to take advantage of the potential of intelligent machines) (Meier et al., 2021; Schuetz and Venkatesh, 2020). The fact that learners have limited skill sets and a strong need for continuous learning suggests that organizations should invest more in on-the-job learning and utilize digital learning tools like machine learning and robotics application (González-Pérez and Ramírez-Montoya, 2022). Digitized class platforms, internet-connected gadgets like laptops, tablets, Chromebooks, etc. and cutting-edge virtual reality experiences have emerged as game-changers in providing immersive, interactive, and highly effective learning environments that enable employees to acquire and enhance their skills in a dynamic and engaging manner (Haleem et al., 2022).

Gamification in digital learning has become an exceedingly popular trend in education, creating a delightful and engaging learning experience for students. This innovative approach integrates game mechanics and elements into educational activities to enhance motivation, increase participation, and foster a deeper understanding of academic concepts. By transforming ordinary lessons into interactive challenges and rewarding accomplishments with badges, points, or leaderboards, students are driven to actively pursue knowledge and skills. With the integration of personalized feedback and progress tracking, learners can monitor their development, set goals, and celebrate achievements, reinforcing a sense of accomplishment and continuous improvement (Campillo-Ferrer et al., 2020; Saleem et al., 2021).

Simulations and modeling techniques are invaluable tools that can aid leaders in comprehending intricate scenarios and formulating well-informed decisions that will shape the future of learning organizations. Through the application of simulations and modeling, leaders can gain a deeper understanding and insight into the multifaceted nature of various situations, allowing them to anticipate potential challenges, identify opportunities, and strategize effectively (Hallinger and Wang, 2020).

In the field of education, technologies such as AI, virtual reality, and augmented reality offer personalized learning experiences for students by analyzing large amounts of data and creating immersive virtual environments. Augmented reality enhances real-world environments by overlaying digital information, creating interactive learning experiences. With these tools, education has become more engaging, accessible, and inclusive, leading the way toward a more immersive, interactive, and innovative educational experience in the future (Gandedkar et al., 2021; Al-Ansi et al., 2023).

5. Digital Leadership and Education 4.0: The Transformation of Learning Organizations

Education 4.0 is a revolutionary and innovative approach to learning that introduces a whole new dimension to education. Through Education 4.0, learners are empowered to take responsibility for their learning, develop critical thinking skills, and play an active role in their education (Hımmetoglu et al., 2020; Moraes et al., 2023).

The emergence of digital leadership in Education 4.0 has fundamentally changed the way learning organizations operate, requiring them to embrace and integrate the latest technological advances, innovations, and digital tools (Temelkova, 2020). With the rapid advancement of digital technologies, educational leaders can adapt education to meet student needs and create dynamic, engaging learning environments by leveraging data-driven insights, personalized learning platforms, and collaboration tools (Anak and Sri, 2020; Rane et al., 2023). This requires a strong commitment to ongoing professional development, as well as a deep understanding of the ethical, legal, and societal implications of technology in education (Alenezi, 2023). In order to seize these issues, organizations need to anticipate new training strategies, redefine traditional roles, and develop a mindset of adaptability and innovation. By adopting and implementing this process, organizations can create a more future-ready workforce and stay ahead in an increasingly global and unpredictable world (Bonfield et al., 2020; Ishak and Mansor, 2020).

6. Conclusion and Recommendations

To stay competitive in today's rapidly changing technological environment, companies can use digital learning platforms to empower their employees to continuously learn new skills and knowledge. One of the key benefits of digital learning is its flexibility, which allows individuals to access educational materials and courses at their own convenience. This eliminates the need for productivity interruptions and offers a variety of formats to accommodate different learning styles. Additionally, digital learning provides personalized learning experiences by using data analytics and artificial intelligence to assess individual proficiency levels and adapt learning paths accordingly. It also encourages continuous learning and lifelong development by providing access to up-to-date content, industry-specific expertise, and opportunities for students to connect and collaborate with others. Embracing digital learning can equip organizations with the tools and resources needed to thrive in today's fast-paced business environment.

This is where digital leaders come in, as they play a vital role in driving their organizations to foster a culture of continuous learning. With their proficiency in digital environments, these leaders can leverage the technology needed to drive innovation, increase productivity, and foster collaboration within the organization. The most important feature of these leaders is that they understand the importance of continuous learning and can quickly adapt to changes in the digital environment. By adopting a forward-thinking digital mindset and advocating a culture of digital fluency among employees, these leaders can empower their teams and guide them to success in the digital realm. By being informed about digital trends and encouraging a culture of continuous learning and improvement, organizations can leverage the power of digital leadership to redefine their strategies and revolutionize their approaches.

References

Ahlquist, J. (2020). *Digital leadership in higher education: Purposeful social media in a connected world*. Routledge.

Al-Ansi, A. M., Jaboob, M., Garad, A., & Al-Ansi, A. (2023). Analyzing augmented reality (AR) and virtual reality (VR) recent development in education. *Social Sciences & Humanities Open*, *8*(1), 100532.

Alenezi, M. (2023). Digital learning and digital institution in higher education. *Education Sciences*, *13*(1), 88.

Alerasoul, S. A., Afeltra, G., Hakala, H., Minelli, E., & Strozzi, F. (2022). Organisational learning, learning organisation, and learning orientation: An integrative review and framework. *Human Resource Management Review*, *32*(3), 100854.

Anak Agung Sagung, M. A., & Sri Darma, G. (2020). Revealing the digital leadership spurs in 4.0 industrial revolution. *Asri, AASMANi & Darma, GS, Revealing the digital leadership spurs in*, *4*, 93–100.

Benitez, J., Arenas, A., Castillo, A., & Esteves, J. (2022). Impact of digital leadership capability on innovation performance: The role of platform digitization capability. *Information & Management*, *59*(2), 103590.

Bonfield, C. A., Salter, M., Longmuir, A., Benson, M., & Adachi, C. (2020). Transformation or evolution?: Education 4.0, teaching and learning in the digital age. *Higher education pedagogies*, *5*(1), 223–246.

Campillo-Ferrer, J. M., Miralles-Martínez, P., & Sánchez-Ibáñez, R. (2020). Gamification in higher education: Impact on student motivation and the acquisition of social and civic key competencies. *Sustainability*, *12*(12), 4822.

Chatterjee, S., Chaudhuri, R., Vrontis, D., & Giovando, G. (2023). Digital workplace and organization performance: Moderating role of digital leadership capability. *Journal of Innovation & Knowledge*, *8*(1), 100334.

Erhan, T., Uzunbacak, H. H., & Aydin, E. (2022). From conventional to digital leadership: exploring digitalization of leadership and innovative work behavior. *Management Research Review*, *45*(11), 1524–1543.

Gandedkar, N. H., Wong, M. T., & Darendeliler, M. A. (2021, June). Role of virtual reality (VR), augmented reality (AR) and artificial intelligence (AI) in tertiary education and research of orthodontics: An insight. In *Seminars in Orthodontics* (Vol. 27, No. 2, pp. 69–77). WB Saunders.

González-Pérez, L. I., & Ramírez-Montoya, M. S. (2022). Components of Education 4.0 in 21st century skills frameworks: systematic review. *Sustainability*, *14*(3), 1493.

Haleem, A., Javaid, M., & Singh, R. P. (2024). Perspective of leadership 4.0 in the era of fourth industrial revolution: A comprehensive view. *Journal of Industrial Safety*, 100006.

Haleem, A., Javaid, M., Qadri, M. A., & Suman, R. (2022). Understanding the role of digital technologies in education: A review. *Sustainable operations and computers*, *3*, 275–285.

Hallinger, P., & Wang, R. (2020). The evolution of simulation-based learning across the disciplines, 1965–2018: A science map of the literature. *Simulation & Gaming*, *51*(1), 9–32.

Hımmetoglu, B., Aydug, D., & Bayrak, C. (2020). Education 4.0: Defining the teacher, the student, and the school manager aspects of the revolution. *Turkish Online Journal of Distance Education*, *21*(Special Issue-IODL), 12–28.

Hsu, S. W., & Lamb, P. (2020). Still in search of learning organization? Towards a radical account of The Fifth Discipline: The Art and Practice of the Learning Organization. *The learning organization*, *27*(1), 31–41.

Ishak, R., & Mansor, M. (2020). The relationship between knowledge management and organizational learning with academic staff readiness for education 4.0. *Eurasian Journal of Educational Research*, *20*(85), 169–184.

Ivaldi, S., Scaratti, G., & Fregnan, E. (2022). Dwelling within the fourth industrial revolution: organizational learning for new competences, processes and work cultures. *Journal of Workplace Learning*, *34*(1), 1–26.

Kiron, D., Kane, G. C., Palmer, D., Phillips, A. N., & Buckley, N. (2016). Aligning the organization for its digital future. *MIT Sloan Management Review*, *58*(1).

Klein, M. (2020), Leadership Characteristics in the Era of Digital Transformation, *BMIJ*, 8(1): 883–902.

Konstantinou, E., Nachbagauer, A., & Wehnes, H. (2023). Digital learning and education in a project society. *Project Leadership and Society*, *4*, 100083.

Maheshwari, S. K., & Yadav, J. (2020). Leadership in the digital age: emerging paradigms and challenges. *International Journal of Business and Globalisation*, *26*(3), 220–238.

McCarthy, A. M., Maor, D., McConney, A., & Cavanaugh, C. (2023). Digital transformation in education: Critical components for leaders of system change. *Social Sciences & Humanities Open*, *8*(1), 100479.

McCarthy, P., Sammon, D., & Alhassan, I. (2022). Digital transformation leadership characteristics: A literature analysis. *Journal of Decision Systems*, *32*(1), 79–109.

Meier, C., Seufert, S., Guggemos, J., & Spirgi, J. (2021). Learning organizations in the age of smart machines: fusion skills, augmentation strategies, and the role of HRD professionals. *Digital transformation of learning organizations*, 77–94.

Moraes, E. B., Kipper, L. M., Hackenhaar Kellermann, A. C., Austria, L., Leivas, P., Moraes, J. A. R., & Witczak, M. (2023). Integration of Industry 4.0 technologies with Education 4.0: advantages for improvements in learning. *Interactive Technology and Smart Education*, *20*(2), 271–287.

Musaigwa, M., & Kalitanyi, V. (2024). Effective leadership in the digital era: an exploration of change management. *Technology audit and production reserves*, *1*(4/75), 6–14.

Phakamach, P., Panjarattanakorn, D., & Onsampant, S. (2023). Conceptualization and development of digital leadership to drive corporate digital transformation for sustainable success. *International Journal of Educational Communications and Technology*, *3*(2), 30–42.

Rane, N., Choudhary, S., & Rane, J. (2023). Education 4.0 and 5.0: Integrating artificial intelligence (AI) for personalized and adaptive learning. *Journal Of Artificial Intelligence and Robotics*,1(1),29–43.

Reese, S. (2020). Reflecting on impacts of Peter Senge's Fifth Discipline on learning organizations. *The Learning Organization*, *27*(1), 75–80.

Ruël, H., Rowlands, H., & Njoku, E. (2021). Digital business strategizing: the role of leadership and organizational learning. *Competitiveness Review: An International Business Journal*, *31*(1), 145–161.

Sağbaş, M., & Erdoğan, F. A. (2022). Digital leadership: a systematic conceptual literature review. *İstanbul Kent Üniversitesi İnsan ve Toplum Bilimleri Dergisi*, *3*(1), 17–35.

Saleem, A. N., Noori, N. M., & Ozdamli, F. (2022). Gamification applications in E-learning: A literature review. *Technology, Knowledge and Learning, 27*(1), 139–159.

Schuetz, S., & Venkatesh, V. (2020). The rise of human machines: How cognitive computing systems challenge assumptions of user-system interaction. *Journal of the Association for Information Systems, 21*(2), 460–482.

Sousa, M. J., & Rocha, Á. (2019). Digital learning: Developing skills for digital transformation of organizations. *Future Generation Computer Systems, 91*, 327–334.

Temelkova, M. (2020). Digital Leadership Added Value in the Digital Smart Organizations. *Journal of Engineering Science and Technology Review*, 252–257.

Tortorella, G. L., Vergara, A. M. C., Garza-Reyes, J. A., & Sawhney, R. (2020). Organizational learning paths based upon industry 4.0 adoption: An empirical study with Brazilian manufacturers. *International Journal of Production Economics, 219*, 284–294.

Veithzal, A. P., & Rony, Z. T. (2024). Analysis of Implementing Digital Leadership Within Organizations. *Dinasti International Journal of Digital Business Management, 5*(2), 303–316.

Yansen, Y., & Yujie, Z. (2023). The impact of transformative digital leadership on organizational innovation: a case study of successful digital transformation. *International Journal of Advanced Research in Technology and Innovation, 5*(1), 57–71.

Zaoui, F., & Souissi, N. (2020). Roadmap for digital transformation: A literature review. *Procedia Computer Science, 175*, 621–628.

Zhang, Y., & Zhao, X. (2016). Digital Leadership: The Role of Social Media in Transformational Leadership. *Leadership & Organization Development Journal, 37*(4), 494–507. DOI:10.1108/LODJ-09-2015-0176.

8

The Digital Transformation-Based Strategic Management Processes

Yıldız Yılmaz Güzey[1] *& Hasan Boztoprak*[2]

1. Introduction

Barney (2001: 636) emphasized the importance of technology for sustainable competitive advantage. According to the author, skilled technology users are important for being inimitable. Some researchers within the resource-based view have addressed the dynamic capabilities concept (Teece et al., 1997) starting from the question of how competitive advantage is shaped under rapid and unpredictable environments (Eisenhardt and Martin, 2000: 1106). They are firm's abilities to integrate, build, and reconfigure internal and external competences to address rapidly changing environments (Teece et al., 1997). Particularly with the rise of the digital organization notion (McLaughlin, 2017), adaptation is increasingly recognized as a crucial factor for organizations. In essence, digital transformation is a special kind of strategic response and therefore the digital transformation process is a strategic matter (Rêgo et al., 2021).

The digital transformation forces organizations to develop the appropriate dynamic capabilities that ensure systematically and continuously adaptation to stay competitive to meet environmental change (Schneider et al., 2024: 9095) and to overcome the increasing complexity and flexibility that digital transformation leads (Magistretti et al., 2021: 60).

Based on this theoretical framework, this study attempts to address how digital transformation affects strategic management processes. Scholars know very little about the dynamics of new technologies and their impacts on

1 Prof. Dr., İstanbul Beykent University, <yildizguzey@beykent.edu.tr>
2 Asst. Prof., İstanbul Beykent University, <hasanboztoprak@beykent.edu.tr>

strategic management processes (Troise, 2022: 330). In essence, the digital transformation is also an internal process, where operations aim to respond to the opportunities uncovered by digital technologies (Porfírio et al., 2021: 611). Therefore, it is important to explore the internal dynamics of organizations in order to explain the relationship between strategic management and digital transformation.

2. Digitalization

Digitalization means utilizing the digital technologies to generate and capture value (Gobble, 2018: 56). Technologies such as 5G, IoT, big data, AI, distributed ledger technologies (DLT) and multi-cloud, autonomous vehicles, and three-dimensional (3D) printing offers new possibilities to transform strategy and operations in ways not imagined even a short time ago (Li, 2020: 810). The spread of digital technologies has a major influence on business activities, models, decision-making processes, boundaries, cultures and value chains (Iscaro et al., 2022: 450).

3. Digital Transformation

The digital transformation is a change in the ways that firms exploit digital technologies (Verhoef et al., 2021: 888). So that traditional business models may fail to meet the realities of being a digital organization (Li, 2020: 812). Because digital transformation involves shift in business models including most important operations, products and business processes (Rêgo et al., 2021). It is essentially about becoming a data-driven and highly agile organization (Schank, 2023: 5) and an organizational effort to leverage the new capabilities provided by digital technologies to transform the way organizations conduct their strategies and operations (Li, 2020: 810).

4. Digital Transformation and Strategic Management

The digital transformation has a significant and positive impact on the performance, innovative capability and competitive advantage (Schneider et al., 2024: 9004; Ellström et al., 2021: 273). The digital organizations achieve higher levels of productivity growth, improved customer satisfaction, and more innovative capabilities (Schank, 2023: 6). And it also ensures that organizations allocate their resources more efficiently, prioritizing digital transformation-focused initiatives and investments in dynamic capabilities that have the highest impact on innovation performance (Schneider et al., 2024: 9095).

In another perspective, digital transformation presents a significant survival challenge for modern organizations due to digital disruption (Li, 2020: 809). In fact, organizations that fail to achieve digital transformation are lagging in competition and facing serious survival problems. Warner and Wäger (2019: 344) stated that digital transformation can lead to changes on the business models, collaborative initiations and eventually on the organizational culture.

Digital transformation compels organizations and industries to adopt major changes and critical organizational adaptations if they wish to survive (Porfírio et al., 2021: 610). Therefore, it can be considered a specialized type of strategic change as it transforms value creation in organizations and changes the scope of organizations (Rêgo et al., 2021).

5. Digital Transformation and Strategic Management Processes

Digital transformation facilitates a number of shifts in entrepreneurship and in the strategies, processes and interactions of organizations (Troise, 2022: 329). It leads to process disruptions and causes a process reconfiguration along with process innovation, which refers to radical change in organizational processes (Nadkarni and Prügl, 2021: 236). Because of its disruptive feature, digital transformation forces firms to alter their strategic management insight (Grab et al., 2019). The literature suggests that digital transformation is primarily about strategy, rather than technology, which implies that top leadership teams must find ways to take advantage of new and unexpected business model innovations that optimize customer needs and experiences (Warner and Wäger, 2019: 326). Because technological advancements provide plenty of advantages and therefore technologies have a role in the strategic development of firms (Ellström et al., 2021: 273).

Rêgo and colleagues (2021) carried out a comprehensive literature review to analyze the effect of digital transformation in the strategic management process. Authors classified the studies in the current literature in six categories (external environment analysis, internal environment analysis, strategy formulation, strategy implementation, evaluation and control, and feedback and learning) and summarized them based on this classification. With regard to the external environment analysis, the use of big data, ensuring transparent process management through the use of industry 4.0 technologies and thus developing long-term relationships with stakeholders, and ensuring information security. Regarding the internal environment analysis, it is stated that alignment between the headquarters and subsidiaries, focus on business activities and practical organizational culture are essential for an effective digital transformation. As for strategy formulation, there are practices such as finding solutions to problems with digital technologies, realizing digitalization through interactive change practices in production processes, and overcoming organizational resistance to digital transformation with the use of learning. In the implementation stage of strategies, digital transformation is a reboot of organizational system and carries considerable risks; the use of digital tools to reinforce the alignment between strategy formulation and execution stages; the use of digital tools (databases) in the development of new value-added products and services or in personalized strategies; and the use of information technologies as an ecosystem in organizational business models related to value configuration. For the strategy evaluation stage, digital transformation provides a holistic evaluation structure of industry 4.0 technologies. Finally, regarding the feedback and learning stage, the role of customer data is emphasized, and it is stated that digital technologies increase transparency. Grab et al. (2019) asserted that organizations acquire the capability to respond faster to customer expectations in a turbulent business environment by using big data from various customers in the planning stage. For this, firms need to improve their learning and innovation capabilities by building an organizational culture that enables information sharing and effective communication within the organization.

6. Conclusion

Digital transformation is a significant issue that affects all processes of organizations. Strategic management process is one of the most important of them. Developing technology and other digital transformation components have substantial impacts on every stage of all processes, from internal and external environment scanning to the feedback stage. The Internet, artificial intelligence, robotics, cyber-physical systems, cloud technology and modern applications based on these digital technologies are critical for strategic management processes such as collecting data from the internal and external environment, analyzing this data, developing alternatives and decision-making. They also provide practical tools for the effective implementation of these alternative strategies. It also provides a certain and objective understanding in the monitoring and feedback stages. It also provides important contributions in terms of elements such as coordination, communication, interaction and process monitoring, which are important in the whole strategic management process.

References

Barney, J., Wright, M., & Ketchen Jr, D. J. (2001). The resource-based view of the firm: Ten years after 1991. *Journal of Management, 27*(6), 625–641.

Eisenhardt, K. M., & Martin, J. A. (2000). Dynamic capabilities: what are they?. *Strategic Management Journal, 21*(10-11), 1105–1121.

Ellström, D., Holtström, J., Berg, E., & Josefsson, C. (2021). Dynamic capabilities for digital transformation. *Journal of Strategy and Management, 15*(2), 272–286.

Gobble, M. M. (2018). Digitalization, digitization, and innovation. *Research-Technology Management, 61*(4), 56–59.

Grab, B., Olaru, M., & Gavril, R. M. (2019). The impact of digital transformation on strategic business management. *Ecoforum Journal, 8*(1).

Iscaro, V., Castaldi, L., Maresca, P., & Mazzoni, C. (2022). Digital transformation in the economics of complexity: the role of predictive models in strategic management. *Journal of Strategy and Management, 15*(3), 450–467.

Li, F. (2020). Leading digital transformation: three emerging approaches for managing the transition. *International Journal of Operations & Production Management, 40*(6), 809–817.

Magistretti, S., Pham, C. T. A., & Dell'Era, C. (2021). Enlightening the dynamic capabilities of design thinking in fostering digital transformation. *Industrial Marketing Management, 97*, 59–70.

McLaughlin, S. A. (2017). Dynamic capabilities: taking an emerging technology perspective. *International Journal of Manufacturing Technology and Management, 31*(1–3), 62–81.

Nadkarni, S., & Prügl, R. (2021). Digital transformation: a review, synthesis and opportunities for future research. *Management Review Quarterly, 71*, 233–341.

Porfírio, J. A., Carrilho, T., Felício, J. A., & Jardim, J. (2021). Leadership characteristics and digital transformation. *Journal of Business Research, 124*, 610–619.

Rêgo, B. S., Jayantilal, S., Ferreira, J. J., & Carayannis, E. G. (2021). Digital transformation and strategic management: A systematic review of the literature. *Journal of the Knowledge Economy*, 1–28.

Schank, M. (2023). Digital Transformation Success, Apress Media, New York.

Schneider, M. H., Kanbach, D. K., Kraus, S., & Dabić, M. (2024). Transform me if you can: leveraging dynamic capabilities to manage digital transformation. IEEE Transactions on Engineering Management.

Teece, D. J., Pisano, G., & Shuen, A. (1997). Dynamic capabilities and strategic management. *Strategic Management Journal, 18*(7), 509–533.

Troise, C., Tani, M., Matricano, D., & Ferrara, E. (2022). Guest editorial: Digital transformation, strategic management and entrepreneurial process: dynamics, challenges and opportunities. *Journal of Strategy and Management, 15*(3), 329–334.

Verhoef, P. C., Broekhuizen, T., Bart, Y., Bhattacharya, A., Dong, J. Q., Fabian, N., & Haenlein, M. (2021). Digital transformation: A multidisciplinary reflection and research agenda. *Journal of Business Research, 122*, 889-901.

Warner, K. S., & Wäger, M. (2019). Building dynamic capabilities for digital transformation: An ongoing process of strategic renewal. *Long Range Planning, 52*(3), 326–349.

9

Digital Leadership and Strategic Communication Technology

There's No Better Time than Now

Mehmet Alper Akdemir[1] *& Canan Gamze Bal*[2]

1. Introduction

Today, many businesses, including small enterprises, operate geographically dispersed activities. This requires organizational leaders to significantly adapt their leadership styles (Zaccaro & Bader, 2003:386). Due to the rapid development of communication technologies and digital transformation, managing change has become easier; however, digital leadership remains essential for executing organizational activities. Digital leadership plays a crucial role in integrating digital transformation inputs into existing practices and activities.

Digital leadership is focused on implementing digital transformation within a company. Digitizing work environments and learning cultures is crucial for organizations to remain competitive and survive in the modern day (Sağbaş & Erdoğan, 2022:17). Digital leadership requires a comprehensive and strategic approach aligned with organizational goals (Ahlquist, 2020:75). Digital leaders must seamlessly integrate technology into business strategies (Brown, 2023:42).

The digital transformation of leadership emphasizes strategic social change and the unpredictability of information flow in the digital age. Leaders must be accessible in both the physical and digital realms (Ahlquist, 2020:108). Modern and future leadership heavily relies on communication technology. In internationally scattered enterprises, many leaders and followers interact online rather than face-to-face (Bass & Riggio, 2006:234). Communication is

1 Dr., Ankara Bilim University / Faculty of Humanities and Social Sciences / Department of Management Information Systems
2 Prof. Dr., Kahramanmaraş Sütçü İmam University, <cgbal@ksu.edu.tr>

critical for digital leaders concerning the success of digital transformation processes, the dissemination of innovations, and organizational transformation outcomes (Allen, 2016:163). Traditional leadership approaches are transformed by digital leadership, which uses communication technologies to improve organizational performance and direct strategic initiatives. The rapid change in leadership paradigms focuses on strategic communication technologies, influenced by social media and digital environments, underscoring the need to update traditional leadership research (Ahlquist, 2020:106–107).

The integration of digital leadership and strategic communication technology is not just a trend but a necessity for sustainable success in the modern business environment. There is no better time than now to embrace this paradigm shift and harness its potential for driving organizational excellence.

This chapter aims to elucidate the relationship between digital leadership and strategic communication technologies, projecting their joint development into the future. Initially, the theoretical framework of these concepts will be outlined. Subsequently, the relationship between these concepts, future approaches, and their co-evolution will be discussed. Finally, conclusions and recommendations will be presented.

2. Digital Leadership

The pace of technological development far exceeds its integration into organizational management (Zigurs, 2003:348). Leaders must adopt new approaches, mindsets, and skills due to technological changes (Ahlquist, 2020:74). In this environment, businesses make decisions at a dizzying speed, operating increasingly in volatile, uncertain, complex, and ambiguous conditions (Young, 2021a:2). Moreover, the digital transformation brought about by Industry 4.0 is not just a matter of technology, but it also brings about significant alterations in corporate procedures and organizational structures. The new leadership concept, digital leadership, is expected to assist in this transformation and provide solutions to problems (Klein, 2020:883).

As a social influence process, digital leadership is conducted through information and communication technologies to effect changes in emotions, attitudes, behaviors, performance, and thoughts in organizations, individuals, and groups (Avolio et al., 2000:617). It entails the ability to link platforms to goals to help people (Ahlquist, 2020:12). The mode of interaction is the primary distinction between traditional leadership and digital leadership. Conventional leadership involves direct interpersonal communication, whereas digital leadership relies on information and communication technology for communication (Yoong, 2010:109). Digital leadership refers to a leadership approach that is employed in the online realm, utilizing digital means (Narbona, 2016).

Leaders should utilize new digital tools due to the internet's tribal-like nature. Within this network structure, each user, as an individual within the network, helps to build groups and tribes. These groups require a common reference point. In this context, the leader is the main character, reference, and focal point, closely tied to both the group's structure and dynamics. Through this framework, the digital leadership concept becomes evident (Narbona, 2016:93). Digital leadership has a dynamic and continually evolving nature (Ahlquist, 2020:12). Digital leaders are required to demonstrate agility and adaptability inside the newly established networked organizational structures while also directing the company's digital transformation process (Klein, 2020:883).

Digital leaders facilitate digital transformation in organizations by establishing a clear vision, empowering, inspiring, and motivating staff, appreciating their ideas, and ensuring their active participation in decision-making processes. They design and implement flexible and versatile policies that respond quickly to technological advancements (Sağbaş & Erdoğan, 2022:19). Digital leadership promotes and guides digital transformation using digital hardware, services, and resources; establishes and sustains a digital learning culture; supports and enhances technology-based professional development; ensures digital organizational management; and facilitates and manages digital citizenship (Zhong, 2017:28).

Digital leadership entails the process of reconsidering, reconceptualizing, and revitalizing the concept of leadership within the framework of the technology revolution. It is the ability of individuals or organizations to use digital insight, digital guidance, digital implementation, digital decision-making, and digital thinking to help others, teams, or entire organizations achieve their goals in the digital technology era. Furthermore, it includes the ability to effectively implement global, political, societal, and corporate governance through the use of digital technology (Peng, 2022:216).

The concept of digital leadership is based on the ability of individuals and organizations to use digital technology for thinking and problem-solving in the digital age. Digital thinking aims to produce more efficient, accurate, and intelligent solutions by leveraging the opportunities offered by digital technology. While digital thinking forms the foundation of digital leadership, it is supported by four main features: digital insight, digital decision-making, digital implementation, and digital guidance (Peng, 2022). (1) Digital insight is the ability to accurately identify problems. It is critical to identify problems early and develop solutions using big data analysis and artificial intelligence algorithms. (2) Digital decision-making is the ability to create policies and strategies to solve problems. It is essential for comparing different policy options and selecting the best solution using computer simulations and cloud computing. (3) Digital implementation refers to the capacity to execute identified solutions efficiently. It involves monitoring and auditing implementation processes using applications and blockchain technology. (4) Digital guidance is the ability to shape the environment and gather support in line with strategic goals. Proper guidance enhances the acceptance and effectiveness of policy implementations. It includes analyzing target audiences using big data and ensuring public understanding of policies through virtual and augmented reality technologies.

The characteristics of digital leadership are categorized into three main groups: digital business, social attitude, and general mindset. Digital businesses include digital intelligence, complexity mastery, ambidexterity, digital talent scouting, and business intelligence. A social attitude involves being a motivating coach, a role model, open, socially intelligent, a champion of diversity, democratic in delegation, and employee-oriented. The general mindset involves being ethical, a lifelong learner, knowledge-oriented, decisive, courageous, self-aware, creative, agile, adaptable, an innovative visionary, and possessing networking intelligence. These traits collectively define the essential qualities of digital leaders (Klein, 2020:895).

3. Strategic Communication Technology

Organizations strategically communicate with stakeholders to gain environmental legitimacy. They may invite stakeholders into decision-making processes or address their concerns to build trust and reputation. Strategic communication involves proactive efforts with internal and external stakeholders (Allen, 2016:70–71). It is the deliberate use of communication to fulfill an organization's mission (Hallahan et al., 2007:3). Strategic communication differs from regular public relations in that it prioritizes the key factors that contribute to an organization's success. It goes beyond conventional communication methods to effectively shape the interpretation of interactions with stakeholders (Zerfass & Huck, 2007:107). This type of communication aligns with the overall strategy of the business, aiming to enhance its strategic positioning (Argenti et al., 2005:83).

With the fourth industrial revolution, technological advancements in fields such as mobile internet, cloud technologies, IoT, AI, augmented reality, robotics, nanotechnology, 3D printing, genetics, and biotechnology are accelerating. This has caused a global paradigm shift, increasing the use of digital communication tools (Young, 2021b:14–15). Digital platforms enable real-time interaction with stakeholders, customization of messages, and analytics for communication impact. Kent and Taylor (2016) highlight dialogic communication's importance for enhancing stakeholder relationships. Social media has particularly revolutionized strategic communication by facilitating dynamic and responsive interactions.

According to Schultz et al. (2011), the integration of strategic communication technologies enables organizations to optimize their communication efforts and quickly adapt to changing stakeholder demands. Digital tools like big data analytics and social media help organizations target their messages more effectively and engage with stakeholders more deeply. These technological developments enable organizations to develop a more dynamic and responsive communication strategy, contributing to improved communication outcomes.

Organizations aim to transfer best practices and lessons learned, enhance customer responsiveness, better integrate supply chains, and reduce knowledge losses using digital technologies like expertise directories, collaboration software, email, video conferencing, social technology platforms, and document databases (van Knippenberg, 2015:650).

The components of strategic communication technologies can be expressed in four main categories: (1) Information Management Systems: These are software and hardware systems used for collecting, storing, processing, and distributing information. For example, customer relationship management (CRM) systems manage customer-related information (Laudon & Laudon, 2020, pp. 54–56). (2) Digital Marketing Tools: Technologies supporting digital marketing strategies like search engine optimization (SEO), content marketing, email marketing, and social media marketing. These tools enhance an organization's interaction with its target audiences (Chaffey & Ellis-Chadwick, 2016). (3) Social Media Platforms: Platforms like Facebook, Twitter, and LinkedIn enable organizations to reach a wide audience and receive instant feedback. These platforms are used to increase brand awareness and strengthen customer loyalty (Kaplan & Haenlein, 2010, pp. 61–63). (4) Data Analytics and Big Data: Big data analytics transforms large and complex data sets into meaningful information, helping organizations better understand market trends and customer behaviors (Chen, Chiang, & Storey, 2012). These categories collectively contribute to the broader practice of strategic communication, which encompasses six related disciplines: management, marketing, public relations, technical communication, political communication, and information and social marketing campaigns (Hallahan et al., 2007:3).

Strategic communication technologies have numerous positive effects on organizations: (1) They increase organizational efficiency by automating business processes and accelerating information flow, saving time and costs (Davenport et al., 2017). (2) Information management systems and data analytics tools help organizations make more informed and accurate decisions, providing a competitive advantage (Brynjolfsson & McAfee, 2014). (3) Digital marketing tools and social media platforms allow organizations to build closer relationships with customers, increasing customer satisfaction and loyalty (Kotler et al., 2019).

Currently, the difficulty lies in making decisions when there is an excessive amount of information available, rather than a lack of it. Organizations are increasingly utilizing advanced information and communication technologies to effectively manage the skills and experiences of their personnel. These tools also facilitate the exchange of knowledge across global operations and help acquire external perspectives, essential for innovation and survival (Van Knippenberg et al., 2015:650). In the future, organizations will need to strategically employ communication technology in order to manage information overload, promote innovation, and ensure their survival.

4. Digital Leadership and Strategic Communication Technology

Communication, as a channel of message transmission, is the core component of interactions between leaders and followers. From a strategic perspective, leadership communication is essential for any organization's success. To promote organizational growth and provide operational flexibility, it defines meaning, develops trust, establishes reputation, and manages symbolic interactions with internal and external stakeholders (Zerfass & Huck, 2007).

While the speed and direction of technological capabilities cannot be predicted (Zigurs, 2003:348), new technologies are critical for economic survival (Zerfass & Huck, 2007:108). Recent technological advancements have created new industries, disrupted old ones, and rapidly established communication networks (Young, 2021b:19). Strategic communication technology creates sophisticated communication environments that facilitate easier collaboration between leaders and followers (Yoong, 2010:66) and promote innovation (Zerfass & Huck, 2007:107).

Today's dynamic and turbulent environment necessitates managing constant change and promoting digitalization (Young, 2021:142). Digitalization has profoundly altered how companies communicate, manufacture, and organize (Bolte et al., 2018:637). Therefore, digital leadership requires a comprehensive and strategic approach aligned with organizational goals (Ahlquist, 2020:75). One of the most critical decisions that digital leaders will make is about the ethical and strategic use and application of future digital communication technologies (Young, 2021:142). Van Knippenberg et al. (2015) note that effective digital leaders use communication technologies to align their teams with organizational goals, encourage innovation, and enhance performance. These leaders use digital platforms to create a sense of shared purpose and direction, facilitate collaboration, and support collective problem-solving. Additionally, digital leaders increase their visibility and accessibility through communication technologies, becoming closer and more responsive to their teams.

Nowadays, leader-follower relationships are largely maintained through electronic communication (Bass & Riggio, 2006:222), as communication technologies have the potential to equalize status differences arising from traditional face-to-face cues like appearance, presence, and tone of voice (Zigurs,

2003:339). Furthermore, digital leaders leverage social media to empower and create impact (Ahlquist, 2020:12). To effectively manage the digital landscape, digital leaders must develop specific digital skills. Effective technology management is required for new digital leadership functions, ensuring that the chosen technology meets team members' tasks and communication needs. Electronic communication technologies enhance work efficiency by providing relevant information about activities and team members (Yoong, 2010:109).

Every aspect of digital leadership efforts can be traced back to strategic communication and strategic communication technologies. Ahlquist (2014) identified ten core competencies of digital leadership: (1) Establishing virtual limits for oneself in terms of privacy, time management, and general wellbeing (consistency), (2) Cyber conflict resolution and mediation (controversy with society), (3) Digital strategies of decision-making grounded in constructive, authentic, and beneficial activities (citizenship), (4) Establishing a personal learning network (collaboration), (5) Online self-awareness and reflection of the digital profile (self-consciousness), (6) Integrating digital technologies into leadership presence (common purpose), (7) Using social media for social good (citizenship), (8) Building professional, strategic, and career-oriented online branding (commitment), (9) Digital content analysis, distinguishing accurate and quality information from false or misinterpreted data, (10) Awareness of new technology tools and platforms. Many of these core competencies are related to communication, strategic communication, or strategic communication technologies.

Leadership has become a complex process in the digital transformation era, necessitating the effective use of digital communication technologies. Digital leaders not only facilitate information sharing and collaboration through strategic communication technologies, but they also promote innovation to achieve organizational goals. The technological competencies and strategic vision of leaders are crucial for organizational success in the digital age. In the future, digital leaders' challenges and opportunities will be shaped by their ability to use technology ethically and strategically.

5. Conclusions and Recommendations

Digital leadership and strategic communication technology are fundamental to modern organizational success. Digital leaders must combine traditional leadership skills with digital competencies to manage the complexities of the digital environment. Strategic communication technology enhances leadership effectiveness by ensuring timely and transparent communication, encouraging interaction, and supporting decision-making processes. The interdependence of these elements necessitates investment in developing digital leadership capabilities and strategic use of communication technology. Embracing this paradigm shift is crucial for organizational excellence and potential realization.

In conclusion, the following recommendations are provided to support the implementation of digital leadership and strategic communication technologies effectively: (1) Leaders must be confident and adaptable in various environments, particularly online (Ahlquist, 2020:90). (2) Digital technologies can have side effects on society. Leaders should prioritize humanity and incorporate social, environmental, and economic factors into the decision-making process (Young, 2021:143). (3) For digital leaders, adaptability and lifelong learning are essential (Ahlquist, 2020:89). Future leadership training programs should address digital leadership's unique challenges and focus on digital education design tools. These programs should help leaders develop competencies in digital communication, conflict management, and team relations (Zaccaro & Bader, 2003:387). (4) Rapid and effective assimilation of new technologies into management practice is crucial (Zigurs, 2003:348). Leaders should emphasize the impact of technology and change on business and society. Additionally, they need to be able to implement a strategic roadmap to address these issues (Young, 2021b:19–20). (5) Digital leaders should use social media to create empowerment and impact online (Ahlquist, 2020:12). (6) The extraordinary changes in information and communication technology should be directed toward activities aimed at empowering customers and other stakeholders (Young, 2021b:19–20). (7) Senior executives must be involved in strategic communication efforts. The CEO and other top leaders, including the CFO, should understand the importance of communication, strategically use communication strategies with all stakeholders, and effectively leverage communication technologies (Argenti et al., 2005:88). (8) Transparent communication tools such as internal chat rooms, regular meetings, or corporate social media are essential for direct communication between employees and managers. These tools make decision-making processes transparent and help achieve the company's mission and goals. Additionally, information sharing and lifelong learning opportunities should be provided through databases and chat rooms (Bolte, 2018:638).

References

Ahlquist, J. (2020). *Digital Leadership: Purposeful Social Media in a Connected World.* Stylus Publishing.

Allen, M. (2016). *Strategic Communication for Sustainable Organizations: Theory and Practice*, Springer International Publishing.

Argenti, P., A., Howell, R., A. & Beck, K., A. (2005). The strategic communication imperative. *MIT Sloan Review*, 46(3), 82–89.

Avolio, B. J., Kahai, S., & Dodge, G. E. (2000). E-leadership. *The Leadership Quarterly*, 11(4), 615–668. DOI:10.1016/S1048–9843(00)00062-X

Bass, B., M. & Riggio, R., E. (2006). *Transformational Leadership (Second Edition).* Lawrence Erlbaum Associates.

Bolte, S., Dehmer, J. & Neimann, J. (2018). Digital leadership 4.0, *Applied Mathematics, Mechanics, and Engineering,* 61(4), 637–646.

Brown, J. W. (2023). *Leading the digital workforce: IT leadership peak performance and agility.* CRC Press.

Brynjolfsson, E., & McAfee, A. (2014). *The Second Machine Age: Work, Progress, and Prosperity in a Time of Brilliant Technologies.* W. W. Norton & Company.

Chaffey, D., & Ellis-Chadwick, F. (2016). *Digital Marketing: Strategy, Implementation and Practice.* Pearson.

Chen, Chiang, & Storey. (2012). Business intelligence and analytics: From big data to big impact. *MIS Quarterly*, 36(4), 1165. DOI:10.2307/41703503

Davenport, T. H., Harris, J. G. & Jeanne, G. (2017). *Competing on Analytics: Updated, with a New Introduction: The New Science of Winning.* Harvard Business Review Press.

Hallahan, K., Holtzhausen, D., van Ruler, B., Verčič, D., & Sriramesh, K. (2007). Defining strategic communication. *International Journal of Strategic Communication*, 1(1), 3–35. DOI:10.1080/15531180701285244

Kaplan, A. M., & Haenlein, M. (2010). Users of the World, Unite! The Challenges and Opportunities of Social Media. *Business Horizons*, 53(1), 59–68. DOI:10.1016/j.bushor.2009.09.003

Kent, M. L., & Taylor, M. (2016). From Homo Economicus to Homo dialogicus: Rethinking social media use in CSR communication. *Public Relations Review*, 42(1), 60–67. DOI:10.1016/j.pubrev.2015.11.003

Klein, M. (2020). Leadership characteristics in the era of digital transformation. *Business & Management Studies: An International Journal*, 8(1), 883–902. DOI:10.15295/bmij.v8i1.1441

Kotler, P., Keller, K., L., Brady, M., Goodman, M. & Hansen, T. (2019). *Marketing Management (4th European Edition)*, Pearson.

Laudon, K. C., & Laudon, J. P. (2020). *Management Information Systems: Managing the Digital Firm*. Pearson.

Narbona, J. (2016). Digital leadership, Twitter and Pope Francis. Church, *Communication and Culture*, 1(1), 90–109. DOI:10.1080/23753234.2016.1181307

Peng, B. (2022). Digital leadership: State governance in the era of digital technology. *Cultures of Science*, 5(4), 210–225. DOI:10.1177/2096608321989835

Sağbaş, M. & Erdoğan, F., A. (2022). Digital leadership: a systematic conceptual literature review, *İstanbul Kent Üniversitesi İnsan ve Toplum Bilimleri Dergisi*. 3(1), 17–36.

Schultz, F., Utz, S., & Göritz, A. (2011). Is the medium the message? Perceptions of and reactions to crisis communication via twitter, blogs and traditional media. *Public Relations Review*, 37(1), 20–27.

van Knippenberg, D., Dahlander, L., Haas, M., & George, G. (2015). Information, attention, and decision making. *Academy of Management Journal*, 63(2), 432–439. DOI:10.5465/amj.2015.4003

Yoong, P. (2010). *Leadership in the Digital Enterprise: Issues and Challenges*, Business Science Reference.

Young, J. (2021). *The Leader as a Digital Sage*. In Leadership Resilience in a Digital Age (pp. 142–152). Routledge. DOI:10.4324/9780367280970-11

Young, J. (2021a). *The Journey*. In Leadership Resilience in a Digital Age (pp. 1–13). Routledge. DOI:10.4324/9780367280970-1

Young, J. (2021b). *The Digital Age*. In Leadership Resilience in a Digital Age (pp. 14–27). Routledge. DOI:10.4324/9780367280970-2

Zaccaro, S. J., & Bader, P. (2003). E-Leadership and the challenges of leading E-teams: Minimizing the bad and maximizing the good. *Organizational Dynamics*, 31(4), 377–387. DOI:10.1016/S0090-2616(02)00129-8

Zerfass, A., & Huck, S. (2007). Innovation, communication, and leadership: new developments in strategic communication. *International Journal of Strategic Communication*, 1(2), 107–122. DOI:10.1080/15531180701298908

Zhong, L. (2017). Indicators of digital leadership in the context of K-12 education. *Journal of Educational Technology Development and Exchange*, 10(1). DOI:10.18785/jetde.1001.03

Zigurs, I. (2003). Leadership in virtual teams: Oxymoron or opportunity? *Organizational Dynamics*, 31(4), 339–351. DOI:10.1016/S0090-2616(02)00132-8

10

Leadership in the Age of Digital Transformation

Essential Skills and Talent Management Strategies

Ethem Topçuoğlu[1] & Murat Sağbaş[2]

1. Introduction

The information age challenges established doctrines, redefining concepts like global, sustainable, innovative, and digital. In corporate structures, this era demands new intellectual capital to optimize automation processes, emphasizing leadership qualities. Digital-era leaders must prioritize the collective, spearhead digital revolution, and guide followers through change. This study examines the relationship between digital leadership and talent management, highlighting the role of digital competencies in organizational success. It analyzes the importance of adaptability, visionary thinking, and technological proficiency in shaping future leadership, providing insights into strategies required for leadership in a digitally driven environment.

2. The Scope of Digital Leadership

The digital revolution is driven by the interplay between human behavior and technology within organizational networks. Forward-thinking organizations manage this transformative power by prioritizing sustainability and competitiveness. Foerster-Metz et al. (2018) explored digitalization's impact on leadership, introducing concepts like business 4.0 and leadership 4.0. Leadership definitions have evolved to reflect complexity and diversity, encompassing influence, motivation, and enabling others toward shared objectives (Reed et al., 2019; Baker, 2022). Digital leadership, characterized by

1 Assoc. Prof., Giresun University School of Civil Aviation, <ethem.topcuoglu@giresun.edu.tr>

2 Assoc. Prof. National Defense University, <muratsagbass@gmail.com>

adaptability and technological fluency, is crucial in modern organizational contexts. Shuang (2024) defines it as influence processes aimed at achieving organizational goals in digital environments. With 58 percent of business activities projected for automation (McKinsey & Company, 2022), workforce innovation is expected. In the contemporary digital business environment, digital leadership has emerged as a critical determinant of organizational success. Concurrently, leaders, who are obligated to adhere to the core beliefs that govern organizational practices, are tasked with a mission regarding digital transformation, not only in their leadership style but also in the manner in which they connect with and inspire their subordinates. The VOPA leadership model, developed by Buhse (2014), synthesizes the essential attributes that leaders, functioning as catalysts for change (Ernst & Young, 2011), require to establish an effective organizational structure across diverse sectors and irrespective of organizational scale.

Digital transformation involves the integration of technologies such as IoT, AI, machine learning (ML), and Big Data (Hendrick, 2017). E-leadership is conceptualized as a process of social influence mediated by Advanced Information Technologies (Avolio et al., 2000). Digital leaders create high levels of energy and commitment among followers by driving change, fostering professional development and encouraging collaboration across departmental boundaries. In addition to the leadership roles described, the NHS has identified several five key skills and qualities that can be developed for leadership in public service: communicating effectively, involving other people in decisions, remaining calm and positive in difficult situations, ensuring fairness in dealing with others, and motivating organizations to benefit society. Digital leadership, which differs from traditional leadership with its concepts of transformation, innovation, and digital culture, fundamentally involves creating high levels of energy and commitment among followers by driving change. In a rapidly changing digital environment where uncertainty and complexity are prevalent, the ability to address challenges and emerge stronger is the defining role of effective digital leadership.

3. The Importance of Digital Skills

Digital skills have become essential in our increasingly digitalized world, profoundly influencing both individual and organizational success. These skills encompass a broad range of abilities, including digital literacy, competence, and computer literacy, which enable individuals to effectively understand and utilize digital information sources. The majority of digital skills definitions are predicated on the concept of digital literacy, which Gilster (1997) defines as "the ability to understand and use information from a variety of sources presented through computers in different ways." Santos and Gomes (2024) selected the concepts of digital literacy, digital competence, and computer literacy to represent digital skills. Digital leadership involves understanding how cloud technologies, mobile devices, big data, and social media transform business operations. Cheng et al. (2024), who argue that the concept has emerged as a result of the "usage gap" in digital media, identify three key dimensions that emphasize the competence required for these skills: use digital resources to learn about technology, information, policies and markets; understanding financial information and providing credit through online platforms; improving everyday life using tools such as smartphone.

Digital skills provide organizations with advantages supporting innovation by increasing strategic sensitivity and adaptability. Key dimensions include using digital resources for learning, understanding financial information online, and improving everyday life with digital tools. Reddy et al. (2020) emphasized that digital capabilities are essential for achieving sustainable development goals in alignment with digital technologies. From a strategic perspective, the components of digital skills facilitate organizational innovation toward the digitization of business models (Li & Sukpasjaroen, 2024). According to a report by the World Economic Forum (2023), the five most prominent emerging skills are creative thinking, analytical thinking, technological literacy, curiosity and lifelong learning, and resilience, flexibility, and agility. In this context, UNESCO categorizes digital skills into three main groups: basic hands-on skills, general skills, and advanced skills. These categories encompass both technical and soft skills. Technical skills include digital literacy, data analysis, and cybersecurity, while soft skills involve communication, teamwork, and problem-solving abilities. Additionally, leadership in the digital age requires specific skills such as digital norm understanding, emotional intelligence, networking, and conflict resolution.

The digital transformation has made basic digital technology knowledge essential in business. However, considering that digital technology is not a panacea for every problem and that the ability to effectively utilize its potential benefits is largely contingent on user capabilities, greater emphasis must be placed on digital competence to ensure digital inclusion and mitigate the digital divide (Park, 2017). Specifically, sectors such as digital social work environments, digital education, and Industry 4.0 are re-evaluating work practices and developing novel approaches to the skills and competencies that will be requisite in the future workforce (Gupta, 2022). Historically, these skills required in the workforce have primarily focused on digital competencies derived from manual and technical skills. The fourth industrial revolution has accelerated this shift, necessitating a workforce that is proficient in digital tools and technologies. The necessity for these digital skills has been characterized by the convergence of the digital, physical, and biological realms through advanced technologies such as AI, IoT, robotics, and big data.

4. Talent Management in the Digital Age

The dynamic human-technology interaction has created a creative boundary within our technological and algorithmic framework. Existing methods, including digital transformation, are inadequate for necessary changes. Human capital reports (Deloitte, 2024) show organizations still view digital as merely new technology applications. Given these findings and digital transformation's impact on business, integrating talent management strategies with this transformation is crucial.

Digital transformation, with its multifaceted potential benefits, influences employees and leadership qualities within organizations, encompassing various application systems and organizational frameworks. This influence elicits resistance in organizational processes and underscores the necessity for establishing guidelines and norms to address change and transformation. Enhancing business success in internal processes is achievable through the development of new organizational capacities. Consequently, leaders must first comprehend the potential implications of digitalization on the organization and internal structures, support individual competencies, and fundamentally implement strategic changes to enhance the coordination of processes and technologies (Desmet et al., 2015). On that note, talent management represents one of the primary challenges confronting organizations, emerging as a critical factor in addressing the global demand for human capital.

The concept of talent management as a corporate success factor originated with the term "war for talent" introduced by McKinsey consultants in 1998 (Michaels et al., 2001). The utilization of a war analogy to discuss talent, also referred to as intellectual capital, reflects the adaptation challenges posed by digitalization on the workforce, as evidenced by enduring concrete outcomes.

Upon examining talent definitions, the concept is associated with behavior, potential ability, heritability, mental and physical capacity, adaptation, and innate characteristics (Ceylan, 2007). Organizations implement talent management practices to develop these attributes, including continuous recruitment, retention, training, talent audits, career planning, performance evaluation, and reward systems. Barney's 1991 work provides a framework for understanding digital talent management's strategic importance. Resource-based Theory (RBT) posits that competitive advantage stems from valuable, rare, inimitable, and non-substitutable resources, with digital talent emerging as a critical resource in the digital age.

5. Skill Building Strategies in Digital Leadership

Effective digital talent management involves acquiring, retaining and integrating these experts into organizational strategy. By aligning digital capabilities with long-term goals, organizations can develop distinctive capabilities that will sustain their competitive advantage. In this context, leadership development programs emerge as a strategic resource for developing employees' skills. Augoustinos et al. (2014) discussed three key components for developing effective digital leaders: internal factors refer to leaders' adaptability and comfort level with ambiguity; development processes refer to experiences supported by digital transformation initiatives; and holding environments refer to organizational contexts that support development. The model emphasizes the importance of disequilibrium, construction of new strategies, and development of meaning structures and competencies.

Barney (1991) presented a management framework that identifies the strategic resources that a firm can utilize to achieve sustainable competitive advantage, termed the Resource Based View. This theory posits that organizations should focus on internal resources rather than the competitive environment to identify sources of competitive advantage, viewing resources as the key to superior firm performance. Skill development and acquisition strategies comprise policies aimed at selecting and developing individuals with skill sets that will lead the organization to success, addressing potential gaps that may arise within these opportunities and challenges. Keeping abreast of innovation refers to acquiring new skills for the current job, that is, upskilling, while reskilling pertains to acquiring new skills for different tasks (Gratton, 2019). These two concepts are critical for the contemporary changing labor market and enhance the productivity, satisfaction, and commitment of both the organization and its employees (Kanoria et al., 2023). Given the global talent gap and employment requirements, there is a growing need for skills for diverse job roles and to improve performance in current positions. Reskilling and upskilling initiatives to address this need enable employees to work more efficiently, increase innovation, and maintain organizational competitiveness. The need for reskilling is particularly evident in the context of automation and artificial intelligence, where traditional roles are being redefined. Research has highlighted that reskilling initiatives are critical for workers displaced by automation, such as truck drivers who are transitioning to alternative occupations (Fossen et al., 2022). This aligns with the findings of the Organization for Economic Co-operation and Development (OECD), which predicts that by 2030 a significant proportion of jobs will be transformed by technology, thus creating a "reskilling emergency" that will require proactive measures to prepare the workforce (Simões, 2021).

6. Conclusion

Organizations must embrace digital transformation, especially in leadership and talent management. This involves integrating innovation, agility, and continuous learning into the organizational culture. Leaders should motivate teams to engage with digital tools and foster experimentation and collaboration. A strategic approach is needed to prepare for the future digital landscape, encompassing leadership practices, talent management, and organizational positioning.

Digital leadership is crucial for navigating complexity, managing technological change, and fostering an adaptable workforce. Organizations must prioritize digital skill development at all levels, particularly for leaders who balance technical competence with inspiring change. Digital transformation requires a comprehensive understanding of human and technological resources, with leaders driving change through adaptability and technological fluency.

The study highlights digital leadership's role in talent management and organizational success. Digital leadership fosters continuous learning and adaptability, crucial for maintaining relevance. The ability to anticipate digital trends and cultivate an agile workforce is key to successful digital leadership. Organizations must integrate digital transformation into core operations, invest in digital competencies, and ensure leaders can address the complexities of the digital age to achieve success in an evolving digital landscape.

References

Augoustinos, M., Walker, I., & Donaghue, N. (2014). *Social cognition: An integrated introduction*. Sage.

Avolio, B. J., Kahai, S., & Dodge, G. E. (2000). E-leadership: Implications for theory, research, and practice. *The leadership quarterly, 11*(4), 615–668.

Baker, E. L. (2022). Influence—a core leadership skill. Journal of Public Health Management and Practice, 28(5), 578–579. DOI:10.1097/phh.0000000000001595

Barney, J. (1991). Special theory forum the resource-based model of the firm: origins, implications, and prospects. *Journal of management, 17*(1), 97–98.

Buhse, W., (2014). Management by Internet: Neue Führungsmodelle für Unternehmen in Zeiten der digitalen Transformation. Kulmbach, Börsenmedien AG. ISBN: 978-3864701726.

Ceylan, N. (2007). İnsan kaynakları yönetiminde yetenek yönetimi ve bir uygulama. Basılmamış Yüksek Lisans Tezi, İstanbul: İ. Ü. Sosyal Bilimler Enstitüsü İşletme Anabilim Dalı, İnsan Kaynakları Yönetimi Bilim Dalı.

Cheng, C., Gao, Q., Ju, K., & Ma, Y. (2024). How digital skills affect farmers' agricultural entrepreneurship? An explanation from factor availability. *Journal of Innovation & Knowledge*, 9(2), 100477.

Deloitte. (2024). 2023 Global human capital trends: Leading in the boundaryless world. *Deloitte Insights*. Retrieved from <https://www2.deloitte.com/content/dam/Deloitte/global/Documents/About-Deloitte/central-europe/ce-global-human-capital-trends.pdf>

Desmet, D., Duncan, E., Scanlan, J., & Singer, M. (2015). Six building blocks for creating a high-performing digital enterprise.

Ernst & Young (2011). The Digitisation of Everything. How Organisations Must Adapt to Changing Customer Behavior, Ernst & Young LLP, London, July.

Fossen, J., Chang, C., Ford, J., Mack, E., & Cotten, S. (2022). Identifying alternative occupations for truck drivers displaced due to autonomous vehicles by leveraging the o*net database. American Behavioral Scientist, 67(14), 1693–1715. DOI:10.1177/00027642221127239

Gilster, P. (1997). Digital literacy. *Seoul Heanaem.*

Gratton, L. C. (2019). New frontiers in re-skilling and upskilling. *MIT Sloan Management Review, 61*(1).

Gupta, A. (2024). Accelerating remote work after COVID-19. *The Center for Growth and Opportunity.*

Hendrick, G. (2017). Operationalizing digital transformation: New insights into making digital transformation work. *Harvard Business Review.*

Kanoria, E., Colaco, S., & Dungrani, D. (2023). The Impact of Upskilling and Reskilling Programs on Job Satisfaction and Employee Retention in the Manufacturing Sector. Rabindra Bharti Journal of Philosophy, XXIV(I), 55–64.

Li, F., & Sukpasjaroen, K. (2024). The impact of the digital capability of college students' new enterprises on business model innovation driven by the digital economy: the mediating effect of digital opportunity discovery. *Journal of Risk and Financial Management, 17*(4), 152.

McKinsey & Company. (2022), "What are Industry 4.0, the Fourth Industrial Revolution, and 4IR?," McKinsey & Company, August 17.

McKinsey Global Institute. (2017). "A future that works: Automation, employment, and productivity." Retrieved from <https://www.mckinsey.com/~/media/mckinsey/featured%20insights/Digital%20Disruption/Harnessing%20automation%20for%20a%20future%20that%20works/MGI-A-future-that-works-Executive-summary.ashx>

Michaels, E., Handfield-Jones, H., & Axelrod, B. (2001). *The war for talent.* Harvard Business Press.

Park, S. (2017). Digital inequalities in rural Australia: A double jeopardy of remoteness and social exclusion. *Journal of Rural Studies, 54*, 399–407

Reddy, P., Sharma, B., & Chaudhary, K. (2020). Digital literacy: A review of literature. *International Journal of Technoethics (IJT), 11*(2), 65–94

Reed, B. N., Klutts, A. M., & Mattingly, T. J. (2019). A systematic review of leadership definitions, competencies, and assessment methods in pharmacy education. American Journal of Pharmaceutical Education, 83(9), 7520. DOI:10.5688/ajpe7520

Santos, M. R., & Gomes, M. M. F. (2024). Lifelong Digital Learning: "Computer Literacy," "Digital Literacy," And "Digital Competence" As Dimensions for Digital Skills. *Revista de Gestão Social e Ambiental*, *18*(1), e04403-e04403.

Shuang, W. (2024). Research Status and Enhancement Path of Executive Digital Leadership in the Context of Enterprise Digital Transformation. *Academic Journal of Business & Management*, 6(3), 152–157.

Simões, A. (2021). Language learning during a pandemic: student engagement and communicative competence development through technology-based activities.. DOI:10.21125/iceri.2021.2153

Ulrike Stefanie Foerster-Metz,Katrin Marquardt, Nina Golowko, Andreas Kompalla and Christian Hell (2018), "Digital Transformation and its Implications on Organizational Behavior" Journal of EU Research in Business, Vol. 2018, Article ID 340873, DOI: 10.5171/2018.340873

World Economic Forum. (2023). The future of jobs report 2023. World Economic Forum. <https://www3.weforum.org/docs/WEF_Future_of_Jobs_2023>

11

Paradigm Shifts in Leadership Expectations

Key Challenges and Digital Leadership in a VUCA Environment

Mustafa Kemal Topçu[1] *& Sinan Babaçoğlu*[2]

1. Introduction

The contemporary business environment is characterized by unprecedented volatility, uncertainty, complexity, and ambiguity (VUCA), which demands a fundamental shift in leadership approaches, particularly in the realm of digital transformation (DT). As technological advancements continue to reshape industries and societies, the role of leadership in guiding organizations through key challenges like rapid technological changes has never been more critical. Digital leadership (DL), defined by the ability to navigate digital ecosystems, foster innovation, and integrate new technologies into organizational processes (Benitez et al., 2022; Lin, 2024), becomes a vital enabler of success in this new environment.

Toward this end, the goal of this study is to explore how DL can effectively address the challenges posed by the VUCA world and how leaders can be equipped to guide their organizations through DT. The research aims to highlight the competencies, strategies, and tools that leaders must adopt to succeed in a world increasingly driven by digital technologies. Furthermore, the paper examines future leadership paradigms that prioritize

1 Assoc. Prof., Defense Management, Senior Auditor & Mentor, ST Strategy and Technology LLC, Türkiye, <mktopcu@ststrateji.com>

2 Asst. Prof., Technology Management, OSTIM Technic University, Türkiye, <sinan.babacoglus@ostimteknik.edu.tr>

agility, data-driven decision-making, and the fostering of a culture of continuous learning and innovation.

Within this context, the structure of this chapter is as follows: first, the VUCA concept and its relevance to DL are introduced. Next, the competencies required for leading in a VUCA world are explored, followed by an analysis of current DT trends and their implications for leadership. The discussion then moves to future leadership paradigms, providing a framework for the capabilities and mindset needed to thrive in the digital age. Finally, the chapter concludes with practical recommendations for fostering DL within organizations, offering insights into how leadership development programs can be aligned with digital transformation goals.

2. Digital Leadership Context

In literature, we face two basic digital perspectives as competency and behavioral on DL definition (Lin, 2024). Competency perspective can be characterized as the ability to provide a creative environment by optimizing technical and digital capabilities (Sandell, 2013), the ability on managing VUCA environment (Zhu, 2015), leaders' vision creativity (Larjovuori vd., 2016), ability to enhance sustainable competitive advantage (Duan, 2020), capability to involve senior management and encourage organization staff in internalizing the digital technology (Saputra vd., 2021), and capability to take digital technology to integrate their own culture (Ju, 2021). Behavioral perspective can be defined as do the right things in digitalization (El Sawy vd., 2020), integrating the digital capabilities with digital culture (Rudito & Sinaga, 2017), using technological solutions in work (Najifar & KURTAY, 2018), and combining leadership skills and digital capabilities in benefit optimization to increase business performance (Wasono & Furinto, 2018).

Lin (2024) has summarized the key characteristics of DL as vision, thinking deep, digital skills, network collaboration, creativity, entrepreneurship, digital knowledge, agility, risk taking, digital literacy, adaptability, technology leadership, and flexibility. In this study, DL topic is highlighted in three different contexts as school education context, government governance context and also business management context.

3. Conceptual Discussion and Impacts of the VUCA Environment

The VUCA concept, originally coined by the U. S. Army in the post-World War II era, was used to describe the increasing difficulty of prediction and decision-making in complex environments. Today, VUCA has been widely adopted in the business world, particularly after the 2008 U. S. financial crisis, which brought significant economic instability and unpredictability to global markets (Bennet & Lemoine, 2014). The crisis underscored the need for businesses to adapt to rapid changes, and the VUCA framework became a useful tool to describe the new dynamics of the business environment.

4. Leadership Strategies and Approaches in a VUCA Environment

4.1 Volatility and Leadership

Volatility refers to the speed and unpredictability of change. The 2008 crisis, for example, highlighted how quickly financial markets could collapse, affecting industries worldwide. Another key example is the COVID-19 pandemic, which disrupted global supply chains, altered consumer behavior, and forced industries to pivot almost overnight. The role of the leaders is to influence key variables and decisions to stabilize the fluctuations in the market or VUCA environment in compliance with the interests of all stakeholders.

Leaders are expected to embrace a mindset of continuous learning and agility to be flexible and adaptable in changing and uncertain environments. They can be knowledgeable about emerging trends and be willing to quickly change strategies when conditions warrant. To do this effectively, leaders may focus on creating a culture of resilience in their organizations that encourages experimentation, taking calculated risks, and learning from failures.

4.2 Uncertainty and Leadership

Uncertainty highlights the difficulty in predicting future events, as seen in the uncertainty that surrounded economic recovery post-crisis, forcing businesses to make decisions with incomplete information. Technological disruption is a prime example of uncertainty, especially with the rise of AI and automation. Many industries face an uncertain future regarding how jobs, skills, and workflows will evolve. The role of the leaders is to reduce uncertainty through informed decision-making, scenario planning, and risk management, ensuring that the organization is better prepared for unexpected events.

4.3 Complexity and Leadership

Complexity represents the interdependence of various factors within the environment. In a post-crisis world, global supply chains, regulations, and market conditions have become increasingly interconnected, adding layers of complexity to decision-making. Climate change provides a prime example of complexity in business. Addressing environmental impacts involves a web of stakeholders, including governments, corporations, NGOs, and consumers. The role of the leaders is to simplify the organization and the environment and make it easy for the stakeholders to understand. Thus, they distill the complexity into actionable insights and clear strategic directions.

4.4 Ambiguity and Leadership

Ambiguity underscores the lack of clarity in interpreting situations and outcomes. The rise of digital platforms, such as cryptocurrencies, is a good example of ambiguity. Despite their growing popularity, the long-term regulatory stance and societal acceptance of these technologies remain unclear, leaving many businesses uncertain about how to engage with or invest in them.

The role of the leaders is to make the information complete and consistent that strategies aligning with stakeholders' interests be identified by interpreting data, making concrete assumptions, and setting clear goals.

4.5 Leadership in a VUCA Environment: Future Trends

As the global business environment continues to evolve under the influence of rapid technological advancements, DL has emerged as a pivotal capability for organizations. DL is not merely about understanding and implementing new technologies; it is about leading cultural and organizational change while integrating digital tools to drive innovation, operational efficiency, and strategic growth. The core of DL lies in the ability to navigate the complexity of digital ecosystems, foster a culture of continuous learning, and ensure that organizations remain agile and competitive in an increasingly VUCA-driven world.

DLs are expected to possess a distinct set of competencies that extend beyond traditional leadership skills. DLs may have a deep understanding of emerging technologies such as artificial intelligence, big data, cloud computing, and blockchain. This knowledge enables them to make informed decisions about technological investments and guide their organizations toward DT.

In a VUCA environment, DLs are expected to be agile, able to pivot strategies quickly in response to market shifts, technological changes, or emerging business trends. Agility involves fostering a culture that embraces change and promotes rapid experimentation and innovation (Kaivo-oja & Lauraeus, 2018).

DLs are supposed to possess the ability to foresee and shape the future. This involves setting a strategic vision that aligns digital initiatives with long-term business goals. Visionary leaders create a shared narrative that inspires their teams to embrace DT as an opportunity rather than a threat. As workforces become increasingly diverse and distributed, DLs must be adept at managing remote and hybrid teams while maintaining inclusiveness and engagement. The ability to lead with empathy ensures that organizational culture remains strong, even in virtual environments. With the rise of digital platforms comes an increase in cybersecurity threats. DLs are expected to be proactive in risk management, ensuring that data protection, privacy, and digital ethics are prioritized within the organization.

5. Conclusion

Looking ahead, the paradigm of leadership is expected to undergo significant transformations as the digital economy matures. Future leadership will require the blending of technological competence with human-centered leadership approaches, emphasizing adaptability, ethical decision-making, and collaborative ecosystems. Future leaders must excel in adaptive leadership, a style that emphasizes flexibility and the ability to lead through uncertainty. In an era where new technologies constantly disrupt traditional business models, leaders will need to quickly adjust strategies, re-skill their workforce, and realign resources in response to changes. As organizations become more decentralized, future leaders will operate within networked ecosystems where collaboration across organizations, industries, and geographies is crucial.

Leaders will focus on building partnerships and leveraging external expertise to drive innovation. This shift from hierarchical to networked structures will require leaders to be facilitators of collaboration rather than controllers of information. With growing awareness of environmental, social, and governance (ESG) issues, future leaders will need to prioritize sustainability and ethical considerations in decision-making. Leaders will be expected to balance profit motives with social responsibility, ensuring their organizations contribute to positive societal outcomes. The integration of AI into decision-making processes will reshape the leadership landscape. Future leaders will use AI to enhance their decision-making capabilities, relying on data analytics and machine learning to gain insights, predict trends, and optimize business performance. However, human judgment will remain critical in balancing the ethical implications of AI-driven decisions. In an increasingly VUCA world, leaders will need to build organizational resilience by fostering cultures that can withstand disruption. Resilience involves not only financial and operational stability but also mental resilience—ensuring that leaders and their teams can adapt, learn, and recover from challenges.

Recommendations

DT is not just a technological upgrade but a fundamental shift in how organizations operate. DLs are expected to employ technology as a key element of their business strategies to drive innovation, efficiency and competitive advantage (Millar et al., 2018). They make informed decisions, predict trends, and personalize customer experiences using technologies such as data analytics, AI, and machine learning. By integrating technologies such as IoT, blockchain and cloud computing, they increase operational efficiency, improve processes and increase collaboration among and between stakeholders.

Leaders are expected to invest in the digital skills of their workforce, ensuring that teams are equipped to work in increasingly digitalized environments. By fostering a collaborative and inclusive work environment, leaders can use diverse perspectives to manage uncertainty more effectively. Giving employees autonomy and ownership over their projects allows them to be more focused on creativity and innovation.

DLs will focus on creating digital ecosystems that enable seamless integration between cross-functional and external partners through technology. To stay ahead of technological advances, they will adopt agile methodologies and foster a culture of continuous learning. Cybersecurity and data privacy will be a priority, and leaders will ensure that technological integrations comply with ethical standards and regulatory requirements.

Leaders are to be expected to develop contingency-based strategies and plans that predict potential disruptions, thus being prepared for possible outcomes.

Innovation often involves a process of trial and error. Leaders must create an environment where failure is viewed as a learning opportunity rather than a setback. By reducing the fear of failure, employees are more likely to experiment with new ideas and approaches.

Employing technology to monitor and improve sustainability performance. Innovations such as data analytics, artificial intelligence, and IoT can help leaders monitor environmental impacts and optimize resource use.

Future leaders are expected to use data analysis and data-driven decision-making to increase organizational performance, optimize operations and drive innovation. Future leaders rely on data analysis to make well-informed decisions. By analyzing large data sets, they can identify trends, patterns, and insights that provide a solid foundation for strategic choices. This approach enables more accurate and effective decisions to be made by reducing dependence on intuition and guessing.

Leaders become more inclined to monitor key performance indicators (KPIs) and operational metrics using real-time data analysis. This enables them to respond quickly to changes in the market, customer behavior or internal processes and enable more agile and faster management.

Using predictive analytics, future leaders are able to predict future trends and outcomes based on historical data. This capability is critical in areas such as demand forecasting, risk management and resource allocation, helping leaders anticipate challenges and seize opportunities.

Using data, leaders identify inefficiencies and optimize business processes. This may include areas such as improving supply chains, improving inventory management or increasing workforce productivity. Data analysis will help leaders identify areas where resources can be allocated more effectively.

Future leaders integrate advanced decision-making tools powered by AI and ML. These tools analyze large amounts of data, providing leaders with predictive insights and recommendations to make better decisions.

Leaders foster a data-driven culture in their organizations and encourage all employees to make their decisions based on data. This includes providing training in data literacy and investing in the necessary tools and technologies for data analysis across the organization.

As data becomes central to decision-making processes, future leaders must ensure that data is used ethically and responsibly. This includes protecting customer privacy, ensuring data security and complying with regulatory requirements.

The field of data analytics is constantly evolving. Future leaders will stay at the forefront by staying informed about new data tools, techniques, and best practices.

Future leaders who embrace data analysis and data-driven decision-making are better equipped to better navigate complex business environments, drive growth, and maintain competitive advantage.

Technology will play a central role in supporting flexible working models. Leaders use digital tools and platforms to facilitate communication, collaboration, and project management across dispersed teams. This includes ensuring seamless workflow and connectivity through the use of video conferencing, cloud-based project management tools and collaboration platforms.

AI and automation can be integrated into leadership processes in a variety of ways, improving decision-making processes, streamlining operations, and fostering innovation.

By analyzing large amounts of data, AI can provide leaders with actionable insights, helping them make more informed decisions. AI-powered predictive analytics can predict trends, identify potential risks and uncover opportunities, enabling leaders to make proactive and strategic choices.

Automation can handle repetitive and time-consuming tasks, allowing leaders to focus on more strategic activities. For example, AI-powered tools allow leaders to allocate their time and resources more effectively by automating tasks such as scheduling, data entry, and report generation.

AI and automation can optimize operational efficiency by streamlining workflows and reducing errors. Leaders can use AI to monitor and manage supply chains, inventory levels, and manufacturing processes, ensuring operations run smoothly and cost-effectively.

AI-powered analytics tools can provide leaders with real-time insights into team performance, project progress, and organizational health. This allows leaders to identify and address issues quickly, ensuring teams stay on track to achieve their goals.

AI can help leaders identify new trends and technologies that may impact their industries. By analyzing market data, AI can provide leaders with patterns and innovations they can evaluate to stay ahead of the competition.

References

Benitez, J., Arenas, A., Castillo, A., & Esteves, J. (2022). Impact of digital leadership capability on innovation performance: The role of platform digitization capability. Information & Management, 59(2), 103590.

Bennett, N., Lemoine, G. J. (2014). What a Difference a Word Makes: Understanding Threats to Performance in a VUCA, Business Horizons, 57(3), 311–317.

Duan, K. (2020). Dimension characteristics and improvement path of leadership in the digital age. Leadership Science, 16, 60–62.

El Sawy, O. A., Kræmmergaard, P., Amsinck, H., & Vinther, A. L. (2020). How LEGO built the foundations and enterprise capabilities for digital leadership. İçinde Strategic information management (ss. 174–201). Routledge.

Ju, Y. P. (2021). Digital leadership matrix analysis and promotion path research in the digital age. Leadership Science, 8, 47–50.

Kaivo-oja, J. R. L., & Lauraeus, I. T. (2018). The VUCA approach as a solution concept to corporate foresight challenges and global technological disruption. foresight, 20(1), 27–49.

Larjovuori, R.-L., Bordi, L., Mäkiniemi, J.-P., & Heikkilä-Tammi, K. (2016). The role of leadership and employee well-being in organizational digitalization. Tiziana Russo-Spenaand Cristina Mele, 1159.

Lin, Q. (2024). Digital leadership: A systematic literature review and future research agenda. European Journal of Innovation Management. DOI:10.1108/EJIM-07-2023-0522

Millar, C. C., Groth, O., & Mahon, J. F. (2018). Management innovation in a VUCA world: Challenges and recommendations. California management review, 61(1), 5–14.

Najifar, P., & Kurtay, C. (2018). Investigation of Availability of Raw Perlite in Refractory Building Material Production. Periodicals of Engineering and Natural Sciences (PEN), 6(1).

Promsri, C. (2019). The developing model of digital leadership for a successful digital transformation. GPH-International Journal of Business Management, 2(08), 01–08.

Rudito, P., & Sinaga, M. F. (2017). Digital mastery, Membangun kepemimpinan digital untuk memenangkan era disrupsi. Gramedia Pustaka Utama.

Sandell, S. (2013). Digital Leadership: How Creativity in Buisness Can Propel Your Brand & Boost Your Results. BookBaby.

Saputra, N., Nugroho, R., Aisyah, H., & Karneli, O. (2021). Digital skill during covid-19: Effects of digital leadership and digital collaboration. Jurnal Aplikasi Manajemen, 19(2), 272–281.

Wasono, L. W., & Furinto, A. (2018). The effect of digital leadership and innovation management for incumbent telecommunication company in the digital disruptive era. International Journal of Engineering and Technology, 7(2.29), 125–130.

Zhu, P. (2015). Digital master: Debunk the myths of enterprise digital maturity. Lulu Publishing Services.

12

The Outcomes of Digital Transformation

Human Resources Management in the Digital World

Yıldız Yılmaz Güzey[1] *& Bahar Akın*[2]

1. Introduction

The term "digitization" was first introduced by Robert Wachal in 1971 in his work titled "The Digitization of Society" and is based on the widespread use of technologies (Halid et al., 2022). Kagermann (2015) defines digitization as a network formed by people and objects and states that this network is created by merging the real and virtual worlds through Information and Communication Technology (ICT). From a human resources management (HRM) perspective, ICT is referred to with terms like web-based human resources, human resources information system (HRIS), and virtual HRM. In this context, the most commonly used term is "e-HRM" (Lengnick-Hall & Moritz, 2003).

Digitization refers to converting physical or analog information into digital format (Gartner Inc., 2018), while digital transformation signifies the restructuring of societal and economic systems through the profound changes brought about by digital technologies. Examples include the transition to remote working arrangements or the complete digitization of banking (Unruh & Kiron, 2017). Digitization is the process of converting physical data to digital form, while digitalization is the broader use of digital technology to transform business models and operations. Digital transformation requires organizations to create appropriate digital metrics and performance indicators to alter business models (Verhoef et al., 2019).

1 Prof. Dr., İstanbul Beykent University, <yildizguzey@beykent.edu.tr>
2 Asst. Prof., İstanbul Topkapı University Department of International Trade and Business, <baharakin@topkapi.edu.tr>

According to Ross (2017), companies can avoid costly mistakes if they understand the distinctions between digital, digitization, and digital transformation effectively. Organizations need to know how they can benefit from technologies such as cloud, IoT, mobility, and accessibility. Digitization facilitates an organization's transition to digital, while digital transformation requires the firm to rethink its value proposition.

According to Bondarouk and Ruël (2009), digital technologies continuously change how organizations hire, manage, and support people. Digital HRM refers to the direct use of information technologies in HR processes within an organization (Matt et al., 2015). These technologies increase employee productivity, enhance the efficiency of employee management systems, and make the organization's competitive edge sustainable. Ketolainen (2018) defines digital HRM as "a process of change aimed at automation and becoming data-driven" and notes that social, mobile, analytics, and cloud (SMAC) technologies are used in digital HRM to optimize processes.

This chapter discusses the practices used in the digital transformation of HRM, the key success factors, and the benefits and challenges of digital transformation.

2. Digital HRM Practices

Academics and practitioners worldwide address digital HRM as an essential management topic. Digitizing HR can accelerate processes like e-recruitment, online training and development, online selection process, rewarding, recognition, and performance appraisal, providing more efficient and faster responses (Ruël & Bondarouk, 2014). Below, seven essentials digitalized HRM practices are explained.

1. **HR Analytics:** HR analytics help organizations systematically identify and measure human factors and make decisions that affect business outcomes (Marler & Boudreau, 2017). HR analytics enable data-driven decisions and enhance organizational effectiveness.
2. **Digital Recruitment and Selection:** Digitization has fundamentally changed recruitment and selection processes. The internet and other digital tools accelerate recruitment processes and provide cost-effectiveness. Digital recruitment involves posting job advertisements online

and allowing candidates to apply through these platforms (Evseeva et al., 2019; Halid et al., 2020).

3. **Digital Human Resource Development (HRD):** Digital HRD includes digital tools and methods to improve employee skills and enhance organizational success. This includes trends such as mobile learning, adaptive learning using artificial intelligence, and personalized training (Dehaze, 2017; Torraco & Lundgren, 2020).
4. **Digital Performance Management:** Digital performance management allows performance appraisal data to be stored and analyzed digitally. These systems facilitate setting performance goals, collecting evaluation results, and providing feedback (DeNisi & Murphy, 2017).
5. **Digital Rewards and Recognition:** Digital rewards and recognition systems enable organizations to recognize employee achievements through digital platforms. This can be done via internal communication platforms and social media (Kavanagh & Johnson, 2017).
6. **Employee Engagement:** Digitization can enhance employee engagement. Digital work environments make it easier for employees to communicate and collaborate. Moreover, digital platforms can regularly measure employee satisfaction and well-being (Lager & Milojkovic, 2018).

Digital HRM applications accelerate and optimize organizational processes and increase employee engagement and performance. However, for this digital transformation to be effectively implemented, some key lessons must be understood.

3. Key Lessons for Successful Digital Transformation

Tabrizi et al. (2019) state that most digital technologies have emerged to enhance operational efficiency and deepen customer relationships. However, if employees do not have the right mindset for change and existing organizational practices are flawed, digital transformation will only magnify these errors. In this context, to help organizations better manage successful digital transformations, the following five key lessons are provided:

1. Define your business strategy: Clarify your business strategy and choose the appropriate digital tools for success in digital transformation.
2. Leverage internal resources: Rather than relying solely on external consultants, utilize the knowledge and experience of internal employees during the transformation process.
3. Design customer experience from the outside and develop transformation plans based on customer feedback to enhance customer satisfaction.
4. Acknowledge employees' fear of displacement: Understand employees' fears of job loss during the digital transformation process and present this process as an opportunity to develop their skills.
5. Incorporate Silicon Valley startup culture: Adopt agile decision-making and rapid prototyping culture to ensure flexibility during the digital transformation (Tabrizi et al., 2019).

In conclusion, digital transformation processes are critical to organizations' long-term success. However, in this process, technological tools and the human factor must be considered. Clearly defining the business strategy, effective use of internal resources, a customer-focused approach, managing employees' concerns, and adopting an agile culture stand out as fundamental elements that will ensure the success of digital transformation. These approaches can help organizations manage their digital transformation processes more effectively and gain a competitive advantage.

4. Benefits of the Digitalization of HRM

The digitalization of HRM has rapidly enhanced organizations' digital performance and created positive effects directly and indirectly. During the COVID-19 pandemic, access to all employees became easier through digital platforms, and HR processes became more efficient, especially during the work-from-home (WFH) period (Luo, 2021). The digital revolution has rapidly changed HR processes, putting pressure on organizations and requiring a swift adaptation process (Ahmed & Ogalo, 2019).

From an environmental performance perspective, digital HRM platforms help reduce waste by significantly decreasing paper consumption and promoting eco-friendly practices (Rao & Holt, 2005). The physical documents used in traditional recruitment processes have improved environmental performance by being sent via email through digital platforms (Halid et al., 2022).

Digital HR facilitates the management of confidential information by ensuring employees access the correct information at the right time. For instance, specific employees can only access certain confidential information. Additionally, managing documents and tracking what content employees read or listen to becomes more efficient with digital HR (Khashman & Al-Ryalat, 2015).

Digital HRM offers solutions for creating an effective communication channel in organizational communication. HR specialists can encourage departments to communicate easily via instant messaging platforms like Microsoft Teams or Slack, and remote workers can stay informed about job changes and provide feedback. This enhanced communication helps resolve conflicts, builds a strong company culture, and strengthens the employer brand (Halid et al., 2022).

The digitalization of HR can enhance the strategic management capacity of an organization. This process encourages HR managers to engage in strategic management planning and motivates employees to actively participate in this digitalization process (Ruël & Bondarouk, 2014). In this way, the digitalization of HR can positively impact improving organizational performance. Additionally, the digitalization of HRM contributes to the sustainability of job performance. This digital platform, used by many large firms worldwide, provides more efficient communication between branches of international organizations and speeds up decision-making processes (Briken et al., 2017).

Digital HRM platforms promote fair behavior by reducing human bias. For example, recruitment processes conducted via digital platforms allow for a more equitable evaluation of candidates' applications (Ahmed & Ogalo, 2019). Moreover, the digitalization process creates efficiency in internal communication by automating information exchange and reporting processes, reducing operating costs, and providing convenience in areas such as teleconferencing and document processing speed. Therefore, integrating digital technology into business processes is considered a critical factor for the survival of contemporary organizations and gaining a competitive advantage (Fenech et al., 2019).

Shah et al. (2017) emphasize that digitalizing HRM processes eliminates many routine tasks, reduces the risk of human error, and allows experts to use their knowledge and skills more effectively to solve significant problems.

To summarize, while the digitalization of HRM offers significant advantages for organizations, it also provides severe improvements in areas such as environmental performance, information management, communication, strategic management capacity, and the sustainability of job performance. This digital transformation creates a fair work environment by reducing human bias and increases organizational competitiveness by enhancing efficiency in internal communication. These innovations brought by digitalization are critical to the future success of organizations.

5. Challenges of Digital HRM

Despite the many advantages of digital technologies, there are also information security and privacy issues. Although big data has the potential to be objective, it can also be highly subjective and contextual. Digital HRM platforms are vulnerable to virus attacks, data loss, hacking, and system failures (Ahmed & Ogalo, 2019). Therefore, it may be essential to keep traditional HRM as a backup to protect privacy and important HRM information in emergencies.

As digitalization takes time to stabilize, sudden changes in HR processes can be challenging for companies (Meske & Junglas, 2020). Additionally, employee inequalities may arise due to unequal access to digital technologies, the experience of using technological tools, and the platform's application (DiMaggio et al., 2004).

Due to technology's blurring of boundaries between work and non-work life, employees use technology for personal purposes, which poses significant security risks. Cyberloafing is when employees engage in activities such as sending individual emails and browsing the internet during office hours (Lim, 2002). These behaviors can decrease job satisfaction and can be seen as a type of procrastination behavior in the workplace (Farivar & Richardson, 2021).

Digital HRM can create challenges such as information overload, increased stress levels, and social isolation. Forcing employees to respond to work-related emails and phone calls during non-working hours can create job stress and an excessive workload on employees (Halid et al., 2022).

Implementing and maintaining digital HRM can be costly, especially for small businesses. Investments in digitalization training and development can create additional costs for the organization (Khashman & Al-Ryalat, 2015).

Digital HRM is a computer-based approach and requires human resources to use this system. In particular, aging communities may be reluctant to try this new digital platform, preventing the organization from fully transitioning to a digital approach (Jin, 2021). The transition from traditional HRM to Digital HRM can be challenging for employees approaching retirement (Connelly et al., 2021). The digital revolution has been a driving force for change in many industries; however, it may take years for such fundamental changes to be fully embraced by organizations and employees.

New technology provides new resources to help employees do their jobs more effectively and efficiently. However, introducing new technology means change, which can create uncertainty and fear among employees, leading to resistance to change. Especially Baby Boomers and Generation X might be more resistant to technological change than Generation Y. Generation Y is accustomed to and uses technology daily. It is rare to teach them how to use a laptop or smartphone; however, previous generations may find this problematic and require additional training (Halid et al., 2022).

Industry 4.0 will change employee roles, responsibilities, and skill requirements, resulting in modifications to HRM practices such as recruitment and selection, training and development, performance management, and employee relocation. Additionally, Industry 4.0 presents challenges for HRM-related job loss due to the need for more necessary skills and qualifications and the implementation of automation, robotics, and information technology (Sung, 2018).

In summary, while digital HRM offers significant opportunities, it also brings many challenges. To cope with the changes brought by digitalization, organizations must focus on strategic planning and employee adaptation. In this process, employees must acquire new skills and refrain from resisting technological change. As the digital revolution shapes the future of HRM, effective management of this transformation will be vital for the long-term success of organizations.

6. Conclusion

In digital HRM, although technology is often seen as a tool that will solve all problems, it should be noted that this approach carries some risks in the long term. Unwanted outcomes such as reduced human interaction, deepening digital divide, and short-term solutions turning into long-term problems may arise (Thite, 2022). The success of technology in project management is not directly determined but is more dependent on organizational and social factors. In this context, success is based on systems thinking, agility, user engagement, and management competence (Thite & Sandhu, 2014).

Looking forward, the success of digital HR will not be limited to optimizing existing digital platforms. Still, it will also depend on the power of technologies to reshape the ways of working and interacting in the workplace. In this context, goals such as creating a flexible and innovation-oriented workforce, fostering a work environment that encourages a culture of continuous learning, and developing an ethical and sustainable workplace will become even more critical (Thite, 2022; Walsh & Volini, 2017). In this regard, successful organizations in the future will be those that not only see technology as a tool but also embrace human-centered digital transformation.

References

Ahmed, A., & Ogalo, H. S. (2019). From HRM to e-HRM: Contemporary developments from scholarly work. *Annals of Contemporary Developments in Management & HR (ACDMHR)*. Print ISSN 2632–7686.

Bondarouk, T. V., & Ruël, H. J. (2009). Electronic human resource management: Challenges in the digital era. *The International Journal of Human Resource Management*, 20(3), 505–514.

Briken, K. (2020). Welcome in the machine: Human-machine relations and knowledge capture. *Capital and Class*, 44(2), 159–171.

Connelly, C. E., Fieseler, C., Cerne, M., Giessner, S. R., & Wong, S. I. (2021). Working in the digitized economy: HRM theory & practice. *Human Resource Management Review*, 31(1), 100762.

Dehaze, A. (2017). The skills imperative: Shaping the future of work through talent and technology. *The Global Talent Competitiveness Index*, 35–41.

DeNisi, A. S., & Murphy, K. R. (2017). Performance appraisal and performance management: 100 years of progress? *Journal of Applied Psychology*, 102(3), 421.

DiMaggio, P., Hargittai, E., Celeste, C., & Shafer, S. (2004). Digital inequality: From unequal access to differentiated use. *Social inequality*, 355–400.

Evseeva, O., Kalchenko, O., Evseeva, S., & Plis, K. (2019). Instruments of human resource management based on digital technologies in Russia. *Atlantis Highlights in Computer Sciences*, 1, 148–154.

Farivar, F., & Richardson, J. (2021). Workplace digitalization and work-nonwork satisfaction: The role of spillover social media. *Behavior & Information Technology*, 40(8), 747–758.

Fenech, R., Baguant, P., & Ivanov, D. (2019). The changing role of human resource management in an era of digital transformation. *Journal of Management Information & Decision Sciences*, 22(2).

Gartner Inc. (2018). Gartner IT glossary—Digitization. <https://www.gartner.com/it-glossary/digitization>

Halid, H., Halim, S. N. A., & Ravesangar, K. (2022). Human resource management practices in the digital era. In *Technological Challenges: The Human Side of the Digital Age* (pp. 109–158). Cham: Springer International Publishing.

Halid, H., Yusoff, Y. M., & Somu, H. (2020, May). The relationship between digital human resource management and organizational performance. In *First ASEAN Business, Environment, and Technology Symposium (ABEATS 2019)* (pp. 96–99). Atlantis Press.

Jin, L. J. (2021, February). Methods, stages, and misunderstandings of digital HR management. In *XV International Conference "Russian Regions in the Focus of Changes" (ICRRFC 2020)* (pp. 82–88). Atlantis Press.

Kagermann, H. (2015). Change through digitization-value creation in the age of industry 4.0. *Management of Permanent Change* (pp. 23–45). Springer Fachmedien Wiesbaden, Wiesbaden.

Kavanagh, M. J., & Johnson, R. D. (Eds.). (2017). *Human resource information systems: Basics, applications, and future directions*. SAGE Publications.

Ketolainen, N. (2018). Digitalization of human resources – The transformation journey into an automated, data-driven service organization.

Khashman, A. M., & Al-Ryalat, H. A. (2015). The impact of electronic human resource management (E-HRM) practices on business performance in Jordanian telecommunications sector: The employees' perspective. *Journal of Management Research, 7*(3), 115–129.

Lager, D., & Milojkovic, E. (2018). Digitalization and the renewal of employee engagement surveys.

Lengnick-Hall, M. L., & Moritz, S. (2003). The impact of e-HR on the human resource management function. *Journal of Labor Research, 24*(3), 365–379.

Lim, V. K. (2002). The IT way of loafing on the job: Cyberloafing, neutralizing, and organizational justice. *Journal of Organizational Behavior: The International Journal of Industrial, Occupational and Organizational Psychology and Behavior, 23*(5), 675–694.

Luo, Y. (2021). New OLI advantages in digital globalization. *International Business Review, 30*(2), 101797.

Marler, J. H., & Boudreau, J. W. (2017). An evidence-based review of HR Analytics. *The International Journal of Human Resource Management, 28*(1), 3–26.

Matt, C., Hess, T., & Benlian, A. (2015). Digital transformation strategies. *Business & information systems engineering, 57*, 339–343.

Meske, C., & Junglas, I. (2020). Investigating the elicitation of employees' support towards digital workplace transformation. *Behavior & Information Technology*, 1–17.

Rao, P., & Holt, D. (2005). Do green supply chains lead to competitiveness and economic performance? *International Journal of Operations & Production Management.*

Ross, J. (2017). Don't confuse digital with digitization. *MIT Sloan Management Review.*

Ruël, H., & Bondarouk, T. (2014). E-HRM research and practice: Facing the challenges ahead. In *Handbook of Strategic e-Business Management* (pp. 633–653). Springer.

Shah, N., Irani, Z., & Sharif, A. M. (2017). Big data in an HR context: Exploring organizational change readiness, employee attitudes, and behaviors. *Journal of Business Research, 70*, 366–378.

Sung, T. K. (2018). Industry 4.0: A Korea perspective. *Technological Forecasting and Social Change, 132*, 40–45.

Tabrizi, B., Lam, E., Girard, K., & Irvin, V. (2019). Digital transformation is not about technology. *Harvard Business Review, 13*(March), 1–6.

Thite, M. (2022). Digital human resource development: where are we? Where should we go and how do we go there?. *Human Resource Development International, 25*(1), 87–103.

Thite, M., & Sandhu, K. (2014). Where is my pay? Critical success factors of a payroll system – A system life cycle approach. *Australasian Journal of Information Systems, 18*(2).

Torraco, R. J., & Lundgren, H. (2020). What HRD is doing—What HRD should be doing: The case for transforming HRD. *Human Resource Development Review, 19*(1), 39–65.

Unruh, G., & Kiron, D. (2017). Digital transformation on purpose. *MIT Sloan Management Review*. <https://sloanreview.mit.edu/article/digital-transformation-on-purpose/>

Verhoef, P. C., Broekhuizen, T., Bart, Y., Bhattacharya, A., Qi Dong, J., Fabian, N. and Haenlein, M. (2019), "Digital transformation: a multidisciplinary reflection and research agenda," Journal of Business Research.

Walsh, B., & Volini, E. (2017). Rewriting the rules for the digital age: 2017 Deloitte global human capital trends.

13

Intrapreneurship and Digital Leadership in Post-hierarchical Management Systems

Hamide Özyürek[1] & Zeynep Baysal[2]

1. Post-Hierarchical Management

In recent years, alternative ways of creating organizational structures with reduced hierarchy have been extensively discussed and efforts to reconstruct organizations have gained significance (Laloux, 2014). Post-hierarchical management has emerged as an alternative to traditional hierarchical management structures, aligning with the needs of modern organizations. This model is described as a more flexible, collaborative, and dynamic organizational structure. Post-hierarchical management aims to facilitate rapid adaptation and innovation by making the organizational structure flatter and more collaborative. It reduces or eliminates numerous management layers present in traditional hierarchical structures (Lee and Edmondson, 2017). This reduction accelerates decision-making processes and enhances communication efficiency. Employees are granted greater autonomy and authority to make their own decisions, and it increases employee motivation, fosters greater commitment to their work, and enhances job satisfaction.

In this management model, self-managing teams are prioritized. Teams work independently to achieve specific goals, with the division of labor occurring among team members rather than managers. Decisions are made collectively by team members, promoting collaboration and coordination. Information sharing and joint effort are fundamental elements that support organizational success (Galagan & Donovan, 1992). Post-hierarchical

1 Assoc. Prof., OSTIM Technical University Department of Business Administration, <hamideozyurek@ostimteknik.edu.tr>
2 Asst. Prof. OSTIM Technical University, <zeynep.baysal@ostimteknik.edu.tr>

management presents a model where traditional management roles are replaced by roles such as coaching, mentoring, and guidance. Leaders are seen as resources that support the success of teams, adopting a more democratic and collective approach in the decision-making process. This approach enables employees to participate more actively in decision-making (Zhu et al., 2022). It provides the ability to respond swiftly to changing market conditions and technologies. Innovative ideas are encouraged, and organizations are continually engaged in efforts to improve and adapt. Continuous learning and development processes are supported, which enhances organizational flexibility.

Post-hierarchical management promotes open communication channels and transparency. Communication is conducted openly and effectively at all levels, improving the flow of information and reducing knowledge gaps within the organization. Employees can comfortably share their ideas and feedback, which enhances organizational performance. Performance management is supported by regular and continuous feedback, facilitating the identification and improvement of development areas. Employees are encouraged to assess their own performance and direct their own development, thereby enhancing their self-management capabilities. This management model is considered an effective approach for enhancing competitive advantage and ensuring sustainable success in the modern business world.

The fundamental principles of post-hierarchical management include the reduction of hierarchical levels, increased participation in decision-making processes, and the independence of teams. The history of this management approach has been shaped in response to evolving organizational needs influenced by industrial revolutions, technological advancements, and changing work environments. Post-hierarchical management aims to make organizational structures more dynamic and innovative, thereby supporting rapid adaptation and innovation processes. The emphasis is on reducing traditional hierarchical levels and adopting flatter structures (Koistinen & Vuori, 2024). This typically involves the formation of team-based organizations and self-managing teams. Team-based structures enhance information flow and collaboration within the organization, facilitating more effective decision-making processes. Self-managing teams can work independently to achieve specific goals and make decisions without the need for managerial intervention. This structure provides a faster and more effective problem-solving capability and ensures a high level of responsibility and autonomy among team members.

One of the most significant advantages of post-hierarchical management is organizational flexibility. This structure provides the ability to respond swiftly to changing technological advancements, thereby fostering innovation. However, the implementation of post-hierarchical management can also encounter certain challenges. The acceptance that post-hierarchical structure brings a transformation at today's organizations and that it only brings advantages to the organizations is contested by some scholars as well (McSweeney, 2006; Prentice, 2022). Role ambiguity may arise when boundaries and responsibilities within the organization are not clearly defined. Additionally, leadership challenges can emerge with the adoption of more egalitarian and coaching-focused leadership approaches, replacing traditional hierarchical structures. These challenges require careful planning and continuous communication for effective implementation.

2. Intrapreneurship

Entrepreneurship encompasses both the creation of new ventures and intrapreneurship. The former refers to taking risks in establishing and managing an independent company, while the latter pertains to employees within an existing company who identify and implement ideas (Hernández-Perlines et al., 2022). Intrapreneurship is the process of promoting innovative thinking and entrepreneurial behavior within organizations (Lara-Bocanegra et al., 2024). This concept can be defined as employees developing new ideas, initiating innovative projects, and improving organizational processes within their areas of responsibility. Intrapreneurship is described as the practice of developing a new venture within an existing organization to exploit a new opportunity and create economic value and it is critical for organizations to survive and maintain their competitive advantage (Parker, 2011; Gawke et al., 2019).

The concept encompasses four distinct dimensions: the first is the new business-venture dimension, which refers to pursuing and engaging in new businesses related to the firm's existing products or markets; the second is the innovation dimension, which pertains to the creation of new products, services, and technologies; the third is the self-renewal dimension, which emphasizes strategy reformulation, reorganization, and organizational change; and finally, the proactiveness dimension, which reflects top management's orientation toward maintaining enhanced competitiveness and includes initiative, risk-taking, competitive aggressiveness, and boldness (Parker, 2011; Antoncic and Hisrich, 2001).

Intrapreneurship helps organizations enhance their competitive advantage, seize market opportunities more effectively, and achieve sustainable growth (Nuryati, Purbasari & Purnomo, 2024). Its general characteristics include a propensity for risk-taking, innovative thinking, the ability to manage one's own projects, and entrepreneurial spirit in individual or group-based initiatives. This approach unleashes the creative potential within the organization and allows employees to develop their entrepreneurial skills.

Fostering a culture of intrapreneurship within an organization involves creating an environment that supports innovation and entrepreneurial thinking. Strategies for building this culture include organizing training programs that encourage employees to think entrepreneurially, supporting innovative projects, and developing a performance management system that rewards entrepreneurial thinking (Deprez, 2024). Additionally, providing open communication channels and a collaborative work environment is crucial for employees to comfortably share their ideas and explore entrepreneurial opportunities. Developing an intrapreneurial culture should be aligned with the organization's overall strategic objectives. One of the key advantages of intrapreneurship is its promotion of innovation and creativity. This encouragement allows employees to question existing processes and develop more effective solutions. Ways to foster innovation and creativity include using creative thinking techniques, rewarding innovative ideas, and organizing various brainstorming sessions. Furthermore, offering employees opportunities to work independently and allowing them to initiate new projects can also promote innovation. Intrapreneurship programs support such creative initiatives, helping the organization remain innovative and competitive.

3. Digital Leadership

Digital leadership refers to the effective use of technology and digital tools in management and leadership processes. This concept encompasses the leadership skills and strategies necessary to adapt to the changes and innovations brought by the digital age. Digital leadership goes beyond traditional leadership approaches by incorporating technology-based decision-making processes, data analysis, and the development of digital strategies. The adoption of digital technologies impacts almost all areas of modern firms, including production, organizational hierarchies, relationships with partners, suppliers, and customers (Vial, 2021). At this point, the role of digital leaders is to guide organizations in the digital world and provide successful leadership throughout this transformation process. This leadership approach is considered essential for organizations to best leverage digital opportunities and quickly adapt to technological changes. According to Sheninger (2019), digital leadership is the ability to initiate sustainable change through access to information, and according to Lyu (2023), it is the ability to use digital technology to obtain and integrate information resources and maintain relationships with members through communication and incentives. Borah et al. (2022) define digital leadership as the ability of a leader to manage the online activities of personnel related to product descriptions, customer inquiries, marketing activities, problem-solving, and decision-making.

The role of the digital leader encompasses establishing a digital organization, including governance, vision, values, structure, culture, and decision-making processes. Digital leadership is a complex structure that aims to create a customer-focused, digitally enabled, and innovative business model by organizing human management, virtual teams, information, communication, and collaboration at the individual level (Jameson, 2022). In digital transformation, digital leadership plays a role in positively developing the relationship between the digital transformation process and business strategies. Digital transformation is the process by which organizations reshape their business models, operations, and customer experiences by integrating digital technologies and processes. Digital leadership plays a crucial role in this transformation process, providing a vision on how technological innovations will be integrated into organizational strategies. Digital leadership has a significant impact on innovative efforts (Abbas et al., 2024).

Digital leaders play a crucial role in the success of digital transformation because they can instill confidence in organizations and employees regarding disruptive and risky initiatives (Abbu, 2022). They define digital transformation strategies, manage technological investments, and ensure that these processes align with organizational goals. Additionally, they help employees adapt to changes brought by digital transformation through effective communication. Digital leaders include both IT leaders with strong business acumen and business leaders with robust, practical digital skills (Benitez et al., 2022).

The tools and technologies digital leaders can leverage include data analytics software, cloud computing platforms, business management systems, and communication tools. By using these tools, digital leaders gain faster access to information, make data-driven decisions, and optimize business processes. These technologies help leaders manage their teams more efficiently and achieve organizational goals. Digital tools enable leaders to conduct performance management, project tracking, and communication processes more transparently and effectively. The skills and abilities digital leaders must possess are critical for adapting to the rapidly changing dynamics of technology. These skills include digital literacy, data analysis and interpretation, technology strategy development, and digital security knowledge. Additionally, digital leaders must have effective communication, change management, and strategic thinking skills. These abilities enable leaders to support organizational success by effectively using digital tools and technologies. Digital leaders excel in managing technology-driven changes and guiding innovation processes with these capabilities. Digital leadership has a positive role in organizational change and innovation, team effectiveness, and employees' creativity and innovation behaviors (Lin, 2024; Zhu et al., 2022).

4. Intrapreneurship and Digital Leadership in Post-Hierarchical Management

Post-hierarchical management provides a foundation for integrating intrapreneurship and digital leadership by offering less hierarchy and more collaboration and flexibility within organizational structures. This approach creates an environment that supports intrapreneurship, while digital leadership represents a leadership style that guides these processes and manages technological changes. Intrapreneurship encourages employees to develop innovative projects and entrepreneurial ideas, while digital leadership ensures that these ideas are supported and implemented with technology-based solutions. This integration, which is often referred to as "digital intrapreneurship," enables organizations to innovate more quickly and utilize technological advancements more effectively (Pinchot & Soltanifar, 2020). The post-hierarchical management structure enhances information flow and collaboration across teams, providing an environment conducive to the effective work of digital leaders and intrapreneurs. It also offers various advantages in terms of organizational flexibility, innovation, and employee engagement. However, the successful implementation of this structure necessitates strong leadership, effective communication, and an appropriate organizational culture (Cunha, Rêgo & Clegg, 2011).

The relationship among intrapreneurship, digital leadership and post-hierarchical management was also studied in empirical research. In a quantitative study conducted by Sağbaş et al. (2023) by surveying 390 participants, a positive significant relationship between digital leadership and innovative behavior was discovered. Another similar study by Gao & Gao (2024) with 359 participants demonstrated that digital leadership influences employee innovative behavior through psychological empowerment. On the other side of the relationship, empirical research also confirmed that a more flexible, flat and therefore post-hierarchical organizational structure fosters a suitable environment for digital leadership and innovation (Kalay & Lynn, 2016; Mello et al., 2012; Reuther, 2016). Therefore, empirical studies also support the claim that there is a positive relationship between digital leadership and innovation which is supported by a flexible environment created by a post-hierarchical structure.

Research indicates that leadership styles have a significant impact on entrepreneurial orientation of employees (Güleryüz et al., 2023; Ekiyor & Dapper, 2019). A democratic and participatory leader that supports open communication and innovation at the workplace may foster an organizational culture of intrapreneurship whereas an autocratic leader figure may repress the entrepreneurial intent of the employees. For instance, a workplace where there is transformational leadership which provides idealized influence, individualized consideration, inspirational motivation and intellectual stimulation (Avolio & Bass, 1995) combined with a post-hierarchical management structure that values individual effort regardless of organizational level, employees would be provided with an atmosphere of openness, creativity and innovation. Digital leadership, on the other hand, works as a catalyst that facilitates the whole process by means of technology and creates an environment conducive to intrapreneurship.

5. Conclusion

The structure of an organization is often regarded as one of the most important determinants of organizational behavior. It is closely related to the leadership style and shapes the way employees act and decide in the organizational context. Post-hierarchical management is a route preferred by participatory leaders who seek to minimize the levels in the organization and seize the potential of each employee with less regard to titles and tags. This type of an organizational structure can be quite fruitful when combined with a digital leader who knows how to use technology to maximize the organizational performance. When used correctly, technology enhances the quality of communication among the members of the organization, enables more flexible yet effective working conditions and leads to satisfaction and fulfillment. In such an environment, employees would be encouraged to make effort, participate in decision-making processes and create extra value for the organization—which leads to intrapreneurship. Therefore, to summarize the relationship among these three constructs, post-hierarchical management is the mindset that creates the environment which is intently related to digital leadership that creates and sustains this structure and together leads to intrapreneurship as an output.

This chapter focused on three concepts as post-hierarchical management, digital leadership and intrapreneurship by explaining how they work and interact with each other. As emergent concepts of today's business world, these constructs can be used in harmony to create more value for organizations by inspiring and encouraging innovation and creativity.

References

Abbas, S. M., Latif, M., & Sarwar, F. (2024). Digital Leadership and Innovative Work Behavior in IT Sector: The Mediating Role of Digital Entrepreneurial Orientation and Digital Organizational Culture. *Employee Responsibilities and Rights Journal*, 1–22. DOI:10.1007/s10672-024-09503-7.

Abbu, H., Mugge, P., Gudergan, G., Hoeborn, G., & Kwiatkowski, A. (2022). Measuring the human dimensions of digital leadership for successful digital transformation. *Research-Technology Management*, *65*(3), 39–49. DO I:10.1080/08956308.2022.2048588.

Antoncic, B., & Hisrich, R. D. (2001). Intrapreneurship: Construct refinement and cross-cultural validation. *Journal of business venturing*, *16*(5), 495–527. DOI:10.1016/S0883-9026(99)00054-3.

Avolio, B. J. & Bass, B. M. (1995). Individual consideration viewed at multiple levels of analysis: A multi-level framework for examining the diffusion of transformational leadership. *Leadership Quarterly*, *6*(2).

Benitez, J., Arenas, A., Castillo, A., & Esteves, J. (2022). Impact of digital leadership capability on innovation performance: The role of platform digitization capability. *Information & Management*, *59*(2), 103590. DOI:10.1016/j.im.2022.103590.

Borah, P. S., Iqbal, S., & Akhtar, S. (2022). Linking social media usage and SME's sustainable performance: The role of digital leadership and innovation capabilities. *Technology in Society*, *68*, 101900. DOI:10.1016/j.techsoc.2022.101900.

Cunha, M. P., Rego, A. & Clegg, S. (2011). Beyond addiction: Hierarchy and other ways of getting strategy done. *European Management Journal*, *29* (6).

Deprez (2024). Intrapreneurship as a Driver of Renewal in Social Organizations. In: Chandan, H. C. (eds) *Social Innovations in Education, Environment, and Healthcare.* IGI Global.

Ekiyor, R. & Dapper, E. (2019). Leadership styles and entrepreneurial orientation, *European Journal of Business and Management, 11* (8).

Gao, P. & Gao, Y. (2024). How Does Digital Leadership Foster Employee Innovative Behavior: A Cognitive–Affective Processing System Perspective. *Behavioral Sciences*, 14, 362. DOI:10.3390/bs14050362.

Galagan, P. A., & Donovan, M. (1992). Beyond hierarchy: the search for high performance. *Training & Development*, *46*(8).

Gawke, J. C., Gorgievski, M. J., & Bakker, A. B. (2019). Measuring intrapreneurship at the individual level: Development and validation of the Employee Intrapreneurship Scale (EIS). *European Management Journal*, *37*(6).

Güleryüz, İ., Sürücü, L., Yıkılmaz, İ. (2023). Dijital liderliğin iç girişimciliğe etkisinde dijital örgüt kültürünün rolü, *İşletme Araştırmaları Dergisi, 15* (3), 1852–1867. 806–817. DOI:10.1016/j.emj.2019.03.001.

Hernández-Perlines, F., Ariza-Montes, A., & Blanco-González-Tejero, C. (2022). Intrapreneurship research: A comprehensive literature review. *Journal of business research*, *153*, 428–444. DOI:10.1016/j.jbusres.2022.08.015.

Jameson, J., Rumyantseva, N., Cai, M., Markowski, M., Essex, R., & McNay, I. (2022). A systematic review and framework for digital leadership research maturity in higher education. *Computers and Education Open*, *3*, 100115.

Kalay, F. & Lynn, G. S. (2016). An Evaluation of Shared Entrepreneurship and Organizational Structures to Increase the Innovative Capacity. *Journal of Business, Economics and Finance, 5*(1).

Koistinen, J. & Vuori, J. (2024). Asymmetries of responsibility in self-managing organization: Authoring shared and hierarchical control. *Leadership*, DOI:10.1177/17427150241264050.

Laloux, F. (2014). *Reinventing organizations* (Vol. 58). Brussels: Nelson Parker.

Lara-Bocanegra, A., Pedragosa, V., García-Fernández, J., & Bohórquez, M. R. (2024). Fit-intrapreneurship in the emerging economy of health and fitness industry. *Journal of Entrepreneurship in Emerging Economies*.

Lee, M. Y., & Edmondson, A. C. (2017). Self-managing organizations: Exploring the limits of less-hierarchical organizing. *Research in organizational behavior, 37*, 35–58. DOI:10.1016/j.riob.2017.10.002.

Lin, Q. (2024). Digital leadership: a systematic literature review and future research agenda. *European Journal of Innovation Management*. DOI:10.1108/EJIM-07-2023-0522.

Lyu, J. (2023). How does digital leadership improve organizational sustainability: Theory and Evidence. *Journal of Cleaner Production*, 140148. DOI:10.1016/j.jclepro.2023.140148.

McSweeney, B. (2006), "Are we living in a post-bureaucratic epoch?," *Journal of Organizational Change Management*, *19*(1), pp. 22, DOI:10.1108/09534810610643668.

Mello, A. M., Marx, R. & Salerno, M. (2012). Organizational structures to support innovation: how do companies decide? *RAI Revista de Administração e Inovação* 9(4).

Nuryati, M. S., Purbasari, R. & Purnomo, M. (2024). Intrapreneurial Innovation in E-Commerce: Driving Fashion Business Growth. ITQAN: *Journal of Islamic Economics, Management, and Finance, 3*(2), 88–94. DOI:10.57053/itqan.v3i2.51

Parker, S. C. (2011). Intrapreneurship or entrepreneurship?. *Journal of business venturing, 26*(1), 19–34. DOI:10.1016/j.jbusvent.2009.07.003.

Pinchot, G., Soltanifar, M. (2021). Digital Intrapreneurship: The Corporate Solution to a Rapid Digitalisation. In: Soltanifar, M., Hughes, M., Göcke, L. (eds) *Digital Entrepreneurship. Future of Business and Finance*. Springer, Cham. DOI:10.1007/978-3-030-53914-6_12.

Prentice, M. M. (2022). *Supercorporate: Distinction and Participation in Post-Hierarchy South Korea*. Stanford University Press.

Reuther, K. (2016). An Evaluation of Shared Entrepreneurship and Organisational Structures to Increase the Innovative Capacity. *Proceedings of the European Conference on Innovation & Entrepreneurship.*

Sağbaş, M., Oktaysoy, O. Topcuoğlu, E., Kaygin, E. & Erdoğan, F. A. (2023) The Mediating Role of Innovative Behavior on the Effect of Digital Leadership on Intrapreneurship Intention and Job Performance. *Behavioral Sciences*, 13, 874. DOI:10.3390/bs13100874

Sheninger, E. (2019). *Digital leadership: Changing paradigms for changing times*. Corwin Press.

Vial, G. (2021). Understanding digital transformation: A review and a research agenda. *Managing digital transformation*, 13–66. DOI:10.1016/j.emj.2022.09.007.

Zhu, J., Zhang, B., Xie, M., & Cao, Q. (2022). Digital leadership and employee creativity: The role of employee job crafting and person-organization fit. *Frontiers in Psychology, 13*, 827057. DOI:10.3389/fpsyg.2022.827057.

14

Digital Leadership

Ethics and Challenges

Arzu Uğurlu Kara[1] *& Enver Aydoğan*[2]

1. Introduction

Digital leadership refers to the skills of leaders responsible for guiding organizations to adapt to digital transformation in an era of rapid technological advancement. However, in this transformation process, leaders face not only technical competencies but also ethical responsibilities. Digital leadership encompasses issues such as data usage in decision-making processes, artificial intelligence, privacy, digital inequality, and the digital well-being of employees. Ethical issues in these areas require leaders to act fairly and transparently, considering their societal and individual impacts (Brown & Treviño, 2006). As the speed and scope of digital transformation increase, the ethical challenges faced by digital leaders become more complex and play a decisive role in the sustainability of organizations (Floridi, 2013). Leaders must model high ethical standards for their employees. Business ethics is currently a significant topic examined in the digital economy. Leaders must establish ethical behaviors to ensure accountable businesses while using digital technologies (Gerbaudo, 2017; Tu & Lu, 2016). Additionally, ethical behaviors in businesses are motivated within the framework of the rule of law and the obligation to be fair.

Studying the ethical aspect of digital leadership is critically important in today's rapidly digitizing world. While digital technologies make leaders'

1 Assoc. Prof., National Defense University, Institute of Land Warfare, Department of Management and Leadership, <augurlukara@gmail.com>

2 Prof. Dr., Ankara Hacı Bayram Veli University Department of Business Administration, <enveraydogan@hbv.edu.tr>

decision-making processes faster and more efficient, conducting these processes within an ethical framework is essential for gaining public trust. Especially issues like data privacy, the use of artificial intelligence, digital discrimination, and cybersecurity require in-depth examination of how digital leaders will tackle ethical decisions. Such a study enables leaders to adopt a more responsible path, considering not only technological innovations but also the societal effects of these innovations (Kane et al., 2015).

Digital leadership based on ethical principles is deemed important because it contributes to the long-term sustainability of businesses. This is because leadership failures in digital transformation often stem from ethical deficiencies, and thus both the opportunities offered by technology and the potential risks and harms must be considered (Floridi, 2013). This study aims to explore the ethical dimension of digital leadership, assisting in the responsible implementation of technological applications at both individual and organizational levels.

2. Ethical Considerations in Digital Leadership

2.1. Digital Ethics

Digital ethics is a field that examines the moral principles and values related to the use of digital technologies. This discipline addresses how individuals and organizations should behave in the digital environment, how data should be protected, how privacy should be ensured, and the impacts of technological innovations on society (Himma & Tavani, 2008). Digital ethics encompasses ethical issues related to topics such as the internet, social media, artificial intelligence, and data analytics (Floridi, 2013).

Key topics in the field of digital ethics include data privacy, cybersecurity, digital equality, misinformation, and the impact of automation on the workforce (Moor, 2005). The ethical principles in this field are necessary to ensure the responsible and fair use of technology (Bynum & Rogerson, 2004). Digital ethics topics can be summarized as follows:

- **Privacy and Data Protection**: With digitization, the capacity to collect, store, and process data has significantly increased. This situation has made the protection of personal data and privacy critical. Ethical issues such as unauthorized use, sale, or misuse of personal data have arisen (Solove,

2004). With the rise of data analytics and artificial intelligence, the protection of personal data has become a primary concern. The collection of data not only affects individual privacy but also societal justice and equality issues (Tüfekci, 2020). This perspective indicates that digitization requires not only a technological transformation but also an ethical transformation. Additionally, Binns (2018) examined in her article how data protection laws (e.g., GDPR) can be integrated with ethical principles, emphasizing the importance of establishing ethical standards to prevent privacy violations.

- **Transparency and Accountability:** Digital platforms and services collect extensive data about users and utilize this data in various ways. Users must be informed about these processes, and there should be transparency regarding how data is used. Furthermore, organizations and leaders must be accountable for the outcomes of their decisions, which is also an ethical necessity (Floridi, 2013). Ethical digital leadership requires transparency in decision-making processes and accountability for the consequences of those decisions. Leaders should openly communicate how technologies are used and the impact of this usage on employees, customers, and society. Data protection laws should be strengthened in terms of accountability, and users' control over their data should be enhanced (Wachter, Middleton, & Leslie, 2021). Crawford and Paglen (2021), in their studies on the transparency of artificial intelligence, emphasized the importance of the traceability and accountability of algorithmic decisions.
- **Access and Equality:** Digitization has significantly increased access to information and resources. However, the issue known as the digital divide, which creates disparities in access to digital technologies among different socioeconomic groups, still exists. Ensuring equal access to digital services and information for all individuals is essential for fair advancement in digitization (Eubanks, 2018). Digital transformation must ensure that all individuals have access to the advantages offered by technology. Leaders should address the digital divide and strive to create fair opportunities for everyone.
- **Cybersecurity:** With digitization, the risk of cyberattacks and security breaches has also increased. This raises the responsibility of individuals and organizations to secure their data. Security breaches can lead to both material and moral damages and should therefore be treated as an ethical

issue (Schneier, 2015). As the frequency of cyberattacks increases and their impact on individuals' privacy rights is evaluated, ethical responsibilities must also be heightened (Zou & Yang, 2022). Protecting the organization from cyber threats is a critical ethical responsibility. Digital leaders must implement robust security measures to protect sensitive information and maintain stakeholders' trust.

2.2. Ethical Approaches in the Digitization Process

2.2.1. Ethical Codes and Principles

Ethical codes are emerging as a critical way to define professional responsibilities and gain user trust (Gotterbarn, 2020). Ethical codes not only provide a legal framework but also shape social norms (Moor, 2020). Ethical codes are rules that guide the behaviors of individuals and organizations, define moral standards, and outline professional responsibilities. These codes enhance the credibility of professional groups by setting ethical expectations and ensuring accountability to society (Velasquez, 2018).

Ethical principles are fundamental values that guide individuals in their decision-making processes. These principles typically include:

- **Honesty:** In the digital environment, honesty is directly related to how individuals and organizations present information and the transparency of their interactions with users (Ghosh & Scott, 2021). In this context, adopting an open and honest approach when digital platforms collect user data increases user trust and creates an ethical environment. Honesty is critical not only for individuals but also for companies; as digitization demands accountability and reliability, dishonesty inevitably leads to reputational loss (Martin, 2020).
- **Justice:** Justice is critical during the design and implementation of digital systems to prevent discrimination and ensure equal opportunities for everyone (Eubanks, 2018). In this context, how digital platforms process users' data and whether they act fairly in this process is of great importance. Justice must ensure that digital tools are accessible not just to certain groups but to all individuals (Sandvig et al., 2014). Thus, justice in the digitization process aims to protect and empower the rights of both individuals and communities.

- **Responsibility:** In the design and use of digital systems, the responsibilities of developers and users require consideration of ethical and societal impacts (Johnson, 2020). This is critical for ensuring data security and protecting user rights. In the digital age, responsibility is not limited to individual actions; it also expresses a collective responsibility that considers the societal impacts of systems (Floridi, 2019). In this context, responsibility in the digitization process encourages both individuals and organizations to act in accordance with ethical principles and enhances societal trust.
- **Respect:** In the digital environment, respect means honoring individuals' consent in the processing of their data, accessing personal information, and interactions (Laufer, 2021). In this context, digital platforms adopting a sensitive approach to users' privacy is a fundamental expression of respect. Respect is an element that builds trust in digital interactions and helps users feel secure (Binns, 2018). Therefore, in the digitization process, respect is crucial for promoting ethical behaviors and healthy interactions.
- **Transparency:** Transparency builds trust by enabling users to understand how digital systems operate and how their data is used (Binns, 2018). This allows users to make informed choices and increases their trust in systems. Digital platforms adopting a transparent communication model is a critical element for accountability and ethical responsibility (Lathrop & Ruma, 2020). Thus, in the digitization process, transparency contributes significantly to raising ethical standards and protecting users' rights.

The implementation of ethical codes and principles helps organizations become more sustainable and trustworthy. These practices not only meet legal requirements but also increase societal benefits (Weaver et al., 1999). Consequently, ethical codes and principles play a critical role in creating a healthy work environment and strengthening relationships with society.

2.2.2. Education and Awareness

Developing digital skills enables individuals to interact more safely and effectively in the online world (Helsper & Eynon, 2013). In this context, education and awareness play a critical role in preparing leaders and their teams for success in the digital world (Kane et al., 2015).

Education in digital leadership enables leaders to understand new technologies and use them strategically. The rapid evolution of technology highlights the need for leaders to engage in continuous learning. In this regard, training programs, workshops, and mentoring opportunities can facilitate the adaptation of leaders to the digital landscape (Baker, 2018). Additionally, by promoting ethical awareness among their teams, leaders can create a more conscious and ethical working environment (Davis, 2020). This is critical for fostering a culture where ethical considerations are integrated into decision-making processes. Leaders should aim to create an environment where ethical discussions are encouraged, ethical dilemmas are openly addressed, and employees feel safe expressing their concerns.

3. Conclusion

Digital leadership requires leaders to navigate ethical challenges arising from digital technologies. As the rapid growth of technology transforms various sectors, ethical principles must guide leaders' decision-making processes to ensure fairness, transparency, and accountability. In this context, understanding the ethical aspects of digital leadership is crucial for fostering an environment of trust and sustainability. Addressing ethical issues in digital leadership not only strengthens organizational resilience but also contributes to broader social welfare.

References

Anderson, R., & Moore, T. (2006). The Economics of Information Security. *Science and Engineering Ethics*, 12(3), 357–366.

Avolio, B. J., & Bass, B. M. (2001). *Developing potential across a full range of Leadership Tm: Cases on transactional and transformational leadership*. Psychology Press.

Binns, R. (2018, January). Fairness in machine learning: Lessons from political philosophy. In *Conference on fairness, accountability and transparency* (pp. 149–159). PMLR.

Brenner, S. W. (2010). *Cybercrime: criminal threats from cyberspace*. Bloomsbury Publishing USA.

Brown, M. E., & Treviño, L. K. (2006). Ethical leadership: A review and future directions. *The leadership quarterly*, 17(6), 595–616.

Bynum, Terrell Ward, & Rogerson, Simon (2024). *Computer Ethics and Professional Responsibility*. Malden, MA: Blackwell Publishing.

Crawford, K., & Paglen, T. (2021). "Excavating AI: Tracing the Roots of the Ethics of AI." *AI & Society*, 36(1), 149–158.

Eubanks, V. (2018). *Automating inequality: How high-tech tools profile, police, and punish the poor.* St. Martin's Press.

Floridi, L. (2013). *The philosophy of information*. OUP Oxford.

Floridi, L. (2019). The Ethics of Digital Well-Being. *Journal of Digital Ethics*, 1(1), 1–10.

Gerbaudo, P. (2017). *Social Media Teams as Digital Vanguards: Leadership in Digital Activism*. Information, Communication & Society, 20(2), 185–202.

González, J., et al. (2020). *Digital Leadership in Education: The Role of Competencies*.

Gordon, L. A., & Loeb, M. P. (2002). The economics of information security investment. *ACM Transactions on Information and System Security (TISSEC)*, *5*(4), 438–457.

Ghosh, A., & Scott, J. (2021). Digital Integrity: The Role of Honesty in Online Interactions. *Journal of Digital Ethics*, 3(1), 15–28.

Gotterbarn, D. (2020). Software Engineering Ethics: A Framework for Decision Making. *Journal of Software Engineering Ethics*, 2(2), 23–35.

Hecklau, F., et al. (2016). Skills and Skills Development in Industry 4.0.

Helsper, E. J., & Eynon, R. (2013). Digital Inclusion and Social Capital: A Social Network Approach. *International Journal of Internet Science*, 8(1), 41–62.

Himma, K. E., & Tavani, H. T. (Eds.). (2008). *The Handbook of Information and Computer Ethics*. Wiley.

Johnson, D. G. (2020). Computer Ethics: A Case-Based Approach. *Journal of Business Ethics*, 162(2), 299–309.

Kane, G. C., Palmer, D., Phillips, A. N., Kiron, D., & Buckley, N. (2015). Strategy, Not Technology, Drives Digital Transformation. MIT Sloan Management Review.

Kuner, C. (2020). "The European General Data Protection Regulation: A Commentary." *International Data Privacy Law*, 10(4), 319–332.

Lathrop, D., & Ruma, L. (2020). *Open Government: A Global Perspective*. 1st ed. GCN Publishing.

Laufer, R. (2021). Respecting User Privacy in the Age of Digital Surveillance. *Journal of Information Ethics*, 30(1), 45–61.

Lessig, L. (2018). Free Culture: how big media uses technology and the law to lock down culture and control creativity. *Communiars: Revista de imagen, artes y educación crítica y social*, (1), 99–108.

Martin, K. (2020). Ethical Implications of Data Collection in the Digital Age. *Business Ethics Quarterly*, 30(4), 589–608.

Moor, J. H. (2005). Why we need better ethics for emerging technologies. *Ethics and information technology*, 7(3), 111–119.

Moor, J. H. (2020). The Ethics of Technology: A Philosophical Introduction. *Technology and Society Magazine*, 39(3), 10–15.

Regan, P. M. (2015). *Legislating Privacy: Technology, Social Values, and Public Policy*. The MIT Press.

Regan, P. M. (2020). Regulating Technology: A New Approach to Data Protection. *Journal of Law and Cyber Warfare*, 9(1), 1–20.

Sandvig, C., Hamilton, K., Karahalios, K., & Lang, A. (2014). "Auditing Algorithms: Research Methods for Detecting Discrimination on Internet Platforms." *Data and Discrimination: Collected Essays*.

Schein, E. H. (2010). *Organizational culture and leadership* (Vol. 2). John Wiley & Sons.

Schneier, B. (2015). *Data and goliath: The hidden battles to collect your data and control your world*. WW Norton & Company.

Solove, D. (2004). *The Digital Person: Technology and Privacy in the Information Age*. New York University Press.

Tavani, H. T. (2007). Ethics and Technology: Controversies, Questions, and Strategies for Ethical Computing.

Tu, Y., & Lu, X. (2016). *Ethical Leadership and Creativity: The Role of Psychological Safety*. Journal of Business Ethics.

Tüfekci, Z. (2020). The Online Competition and the Future of Democracy. *Journal of Democracy*, 31(4), 25–40.

Velasquez, M. G. (2018). *Business ethics: Concepts and cases*. Pearson.

Wachter, S., Middleton, B., & Leslie, I. (2021). "Data Protection by Design and by Default: A Guide for Data Protection Officers." *Computer Law & Security Review*, 39.

Weaver, G. R., et al. (1999). *The Institutionalization of Ethics in Organizations: A Literature Review.*

Westerman, G., Bonnet, D., & McAfee, A. (2014). *Leading digital: Turning technology into business transformation.* Harvard Business Press.

Zarsky, T. (2016). The trouble with algorithmic decisions: An analytic road map to examine efficiency and fairness in automated and opaque decision making. *Science, Technology, & Human Values*, *41*(1), 118–132.

Zou, J., & Yang, Z. (2022). The Ethics of Cybersecurity: Balancing Security and Privacy. *IEEE Security & Privacy*, 20(2), 22–29.

www.ingramcontent.com/pod-product-compliance
Ingram Content Group UK Ltd.
Pitfield, Milton Keynes, MK11 3LW, UK
UKHW020152290926
15471UKWH00005B/830

9 783631 931325